STUDIES IN PHILOSOPHY

III

BUTLER'S ETHICS

by

P. ALLAN CARLSSON

1964

MOUTON & CO.

LONDON THE HAGUE PARIS

Printed in The Netherlands by Mouton & Co, Printers, The Hague

PREFACE

For many years I had been noting references to Bishop Butler in philosophical and theological literature. As is usually the case with many such references, little useful information is given; however, these references aroused my curiosity and the subject was pursued. During the time that I was teaching ethics at both Wheaton College and Trinity College (Chicago), I became increasingly interested in Butler and in the British ethical thinkers of the Eighteenth Century.

While I am responsible for the discussion that follows, I wish to acknowledge that the original form of this material was as a Ph.D. dissertation. The committee for the Philosophy Department at Northwestern University consisted of Robert W. Browning, Paul A. Schilpp, and Eliseo Vivas. I am pleased to have this essay now appear as a volume in this series, "Studies in Philosophy".

The encouragement and assistance of the Virginia Military Institute and of Lloyd J. Davidson, Dean of the Faculty, during the preparation of this volume for publication is greatly appreciated.

Virginia Military Institute
Lexington, Va.

P. ALLAN CARLSSON

TABLE OF CONTENTS

I

INTRODUCTION

How is a philosopher to be interpreted? The answer to this question will contain a philosophy of the history of philosophy. Because of the fruitful ideas which are contained in the writings of many philosophers, it is possible to find divergent ideas which have been noted and used by later philosophies.[1] A study of these divergent ideas is legitimate and of interest since it aids in tracing the history of ideas, but when one possible interpretation is taken as *the* interpretation to the exclusion of the other tendencies, the interpretation can be called into question.

The position maintained here is that a philosopher is to be interpreted by studying the individual, the intellectual age in which he lived, and investigating what he was trying to do. A study of the individual will include biographical highlights, his vocation, his education, and his philosophical ancestors. The intellectual age in which an individual lived is of interest because it often influences his place in the history of thought. A man may remain neutral to the conflicts and ideas of his age, but usually he is reacting by accepting or rejecting them. Few men would have done exactly as they did if they had lived in a different era. To find out what an individual was trying to do is best determined by a sympathetic study of his writings against the background of his person and his age. The way a philosopher

---

[1] Oliver C. Weaver, Jr., "Duty and Purpose in the Ethical Theory of Joseph Butler" (Unpublished Ph. D. dissertation, Dept. of Philosophy, Northwestern University, 1952), is such a study of Butler which shows that aside from any theological consideration, there are tendencies toward ethical hedonism, self-realization, and an ethics of duty which have been claimed by later philosophers.

developed his system is often as important as the result obtained.

In Butler's case it can also be questioned if his philosophy, and especially his ethics, the area under consideration, can be separated from theology. Although it is obvious to anyone who reads Butles that he is using a theological vocabulary, the attempt has been made to formulate Butler's ethics in non-theological language. A recent attempt provides a good illustration; the following statement may be found in Duncan-Jones' *Butler's Moral Philosophy* in the opening paragraph from the chapter division "Butler's characteristic ethical teaching non-theological".

As we have illustrated..., it is possible to extract from Butler's writings a moral philosophy conceived in purely natural terms: that is to say, in which there is, on need be, no mention of the supernatural. This is what his own statement of his method implies: that method starts 'from a matter of fact, namely what the particular nature of man is...; from whence it proceeds to determine what course of life it is which is correspondent to this whole nature'.[2]

Since many philosophers are interested in ethics, but few are interested in theology, such an extraction would allow Butler's ethics to take its place in the history of ethical thought without the encumbrance of the alien theological vocabulary. The assumption of this approach is that Butler's ethics can be departmentalized to the extent that it can be studied and understood apart from the rest of his thought. This separation is made in spite of the fact that Butler has achieved recognition as a Christian apologist as well as an ethical theorist and that presumably there is a certain amount of continuity and harmony in a man's *Weltanschauung*.

In addition to disagreement with the position that Butler's moral philosophy is non-theological, the statement that this is an implication of Butler's own discussion of method is here to be disputed. A careful reading of Butler's whole passage will indicate the appropriateness of raising this challenge.

There are two ways in which the subject of morals may be treated. One begins from inquiring into the abstract relations of things: the other from a matter of fact, namely, what the particular nature of

[2] Austin Duncan-Jones, *Butler's Moral Philosophy* (Harmondsworth: Penguin Books, 1952), p. 142.

man is, its several parts, their economy or constitution; from whence it proceeds to determine what course of life it is, which is correspondent to this whole nature. In the former method the conclusion is expressed thus, that vice is contrary to the nature and reason of things: in the latter, that it is a violation or breaking in upon our own nature. Thus they both lead us to the same thing, our obligations to the practice of virtue; and thus they exceedingly strengthen and enforce each other. The first seems the most direct formal proof, and in some respects the least liable to cavil and dispute: the latter is in a peculiar manner adapted to the several particular relations and circumstances in life.[3]

What Butler really is saying is that there are two different, complementary methods of approaching ethics which lead to the same result – man should practice virtue. If the methods are complementary, one could not be theological and the other nontheological if they are to be consistent. This statement is more naturally understood as an implication of Butler's conception of the universe as an organic whole. In an organic whole, it is possible to start at more than one place and come to the same conclusion.

The assumption that Butler's ethics can be adequately developed and understood apart from his theistic metaphysics is challenged and constitutes the problem to be investigated in this paper. It is fully recognized that the approach illustrated by Duncan-Jones is a very natural one at the present time, since most philosophers are not interested in theistic explanations; but it is also recognized that artificial divisions should not be forced on a man's thinking in order to make it conform to a non-theistic bias. It seems obvious that the recognition of some value in Butler's thought lies at the basis of the attempt to extract his ethics from the rest of his thought; but the question remains whether or not this is a valid interpretation of Butler's historical philosophical position.

In the above quotation Duncan-Jones appeals to Butler's own introduction to the *Sermons* to justify this separation of ethics

---

[3] Joseph Butler, "Introduction to the Analogy", *The Works of Joseph Butler*, Ed. by W. E. Gladstone (Oxford: at the Clarendon Press, 1896), I, 5-6, para. 7. All references to Butler's works are to Gladstone's two volume edition. In all following footnotes the volume number, title of the writing, page, and paragraph number will be given.

from the rest of his philosophy. This introduction along with the
first three sermons is the most widely read section of Butler.
Here he begins with an analysis of the constituents of human
nature, and on the basis of this analysis goes on to determine
the course of life which man should follow. The conclusion is
drawn that since Butler begins with man, the theistic framework
of thought which is most consistently developed in the *Analogy*
does not apply in the *Sermons*. In addition to the fact that this
is a shallow analysis of what Butler is doing, his starting point
can more normally be explained by relating this method to the
purpose of his sermons. Butler's purpose is to exhort his parishioners to virtuous living by showing that their human nature is
constituted for virtuous living; and, inasmuch as such is the case,
the emphasis is on the practical aspects of ethics as opposed to
the theoretical basis, since the man in the pew is seldom concerned with the theoretical basis of anything. The *Sermons* is a
random collection of actual sermons preached by Butler at the
Rolls Chapel; consequently his method of beginning the sermons
is understood to be a homiletical device rather than an implication that his ethics can be divorced from his theistic framework.
This approach which begins with the individual in a space-time
situation and which attempts to draw guides to conduct from the
nature of the individual can be called the psychological approach.

On the other hand, the procedure which will be used in this
paper can be called the logical approach in that it seeks to uncover Butler's theistic position as the metaphysical basis of his
ethical system. It is an attempt to look at his world and life
view through the principles which have a logical priority in his
development. This two-fold procedure is seemingly recognized
by Butler in one of his letters to Clark.

But if you mean, that I first of all prove a being to exist from eternity,
and then, from the reasons of things, prove that such a being must
be eternally necessary, I freely own it. Neither do I conceive it to be
irregular or absurd, for there is a great difference between the order
in which things exist, and the order in which I prove to myself that
they exist.[4]

---

[4] I, "Correspondence with Clarke", Letter III, pp. 424-5.

The psychological approach would be Butler's latter method of following the order of proving to himself the existence of things, whereas the logical approach would be the former which is the order in which things exist.

This study will cover only the theistic principles which have significant implications for an ethical system, since the purpose of this study is the relationship between the theism of Butler and his ethics. Butler would seem to support such an approach in the introduction to the *Analogy*, where he takes for granted that there is an intelligent author of nature who is the natural governor of the world and that this fact should be considered in forming our notions of the constitution and government of the world.[5]

Theism is the metaphysical belief in a supreme being who has created and has sustained the universe, and who may, if he so chooses, be active in the continuing operation of his creation. This embraces in part both the concepts of deism, which stresses the thought of God as a transcendent being separate from the universe he has created, and of pantheism, which stresses God as an immanent being whose activity is limited to the universe. Theism, therefore, combines the deistic idea that God is separate from his creation, and the pantheistic idea that God is continually active within the universe, but does not over-emphasize nor limit God to either of these two aspects.

In our culture and in Butler's, theism is generally associated with Christian theism, but this need not be the case. Butler's development of natural religion in the first half of the *Analogy* happens to be the basic belief shared by all three of the great historical-religious examples of theism: Judaism, Islam, and Christianity. This core belief not only includes a concept of God but also includes certain concepts about man, and may be expressed in three summary statements. (1) There is a God. (2) The human individual is immortal. (3) Life in the future state is to some extent dependent upon the individual's conduct in the present state of existence. In the *Analogy*, Butler assumes the existence of God as has been mentioned above, and develops immortality and the idea of probation in the first half of this

[5] I, "Introduction to the Analogy", pp. 9-10, para. 8-9.

apologetical work. Any man by properly using his reason may know this, and revelation given in the Old Testament and the New Testament reaffirms these principles. The beliefs which make Christian theism distinct from theism are given by special revelation and cannot be ascertained by human reason. This distinctly Christian element centers in the person and work of Jesus Christ and is developed by Butler in the second part of the *Analogy*.

Although the approach used in this study recognizes the priority of metaphysics to ethics in Butler's thought, ethics is recognized as a legitimate discipline. There is a certain manner in which men ought to act. Even though there is an element in the "Dissertation on Virtue" which expresses the idea that virtuous actions are to be done purely for the sake of virtue, this is not contradictory to the main stress of Butler's thought that the individual acts virtuously because this is the nature given man by God in creation and that by acting according to his nature, man prepares himself for happiness in the future life. The main source of motivation for doing what an individual ought to do, i.e., leading a virtuous life, is obvious: this will bring the most desirable results to the individual in the long run – if not in this present life, then surely in the future life. Now for Butler, the same God who has created and has sustained the universe is a moral being who has determined how men should act if they are to be virtuous, and God has so arranged everything that when one lives virtuously, i.e., the way that God has prescribed, one is acting in such a manner as to bring the most desirable results to himself in the long run as well as to bring the most desirable results to his fellow men. This optimistic attitude towards the universe which combines duty and pleasure is developed in the first part of the *Analogy* under the concept of law. Just as there are several laws which govern the behavior of physical objects, so there are moral laws which ought to govern the behavior of moral beings.

The obvious problem which arises at this point is the manner in which the individual is to obtain knowledge concerning the manner in which he should act. Butler thinks that man may obtain some of the necessary knowledge by the proper use of his reason. However, due to the ignorance of man and due to the fact that men may not make proper use of their reason, a special revelation has been given by God himself in the historical person of Jesus of Nazareth, and through the collection of writings contained in the Old Testament and the New Testament. This special written revelation reaffirms the knowledge obtained by a proper use of man's reason in addition to giving information which cannot be ascertained by reason. On the practical side of the matter, Butler has the concept of the human conscience, which is developed in the *Analogy* as the voice of God within the individual and in the *Sermons* as the ruling principle in a hierarchical arrangement of human nature. Although Butler does not make a point of harmonizing these two developments, it is obvious that they are compatible, although, as it has often been pointed out, there seems to be a definite shift in emphasis regarding what the conscience actually does. In the *Analogy* the conscience seems to know intuitively, in the sense of immediate awareness, what is to be done in any particular situation; whereas in the *Sermons,* the conscience works through a reasoning process to obtain this information, in the sense of practical reason as over against speculative reason. In any event, the individual seemingly has several sources of knowledge to indicate his proper conduct.

Just as theism recognizes ethics as a legitimate discipline, it also recognizes metaphysics. Any theism is basically idealistic in the sense that it affirms the existence of another more basic level in addition to the realm of experience with which man interacts, and the Christian theist labels this idealistic realm of existence "God". In the *Analogy* Butler assumes the existence of God as the intelligent author of the universe and the natural governor of the world. Although this assumption would not be acceptable in every age, it seemed to be a natural one for Butler to make in his particular time, since it was maintained by a large percentage of the English population and since any discussion must be within some universe of discourse. In setting the background for Butler's philosophy in Chapter IV, the ethical thinkers

of his age are summarized, and the importance of some conception of God in each one of these systems will be evident.

It could be observed that Christian theism as conceived by
Butler and as sketched above is a coherent system which seemingly is able to account for the facts of the universe; but what
is its advantage over another system such as naturalism, which
is also seemingly able to account for the facts? The philosophical
naturalist would note that by applying Occam's razor, he has
reduced the two explanatory principles of the idealist mentioned
above to only one realm of existence, that of experience, and
therefore, his system would be the simpler. The argument then
hinges on the adequacy of the explanation. In the final analysis
the basis of any system is made by a non-rational choice, although the chooser no doubt may think he has very good reasons
for making his selection. The procedure is very similar to the
manner in which postulates are chosen for any axiomatic system.

There is no intent to imply that the theist has a monopoly on
moral conduct. In fact, a non-theist may act in much the same manner as a theist, although he may have an entirely different motivation for his actions. A consideration which affects motivation and
which is very important in Butler's system is the relative position
assigned to man in the universe. For example, if a non-theistic
position is maintained that man has evolved by a strictly natural
process of selection from lower forms of life and that when his
organism stops functioning this terminates his existence, it is
obvious that the actions of man should be determined by a
standard attainable to some extent in the present life. On the
other hand, if Butler's theistic position is maintained that man
is a special creation of a divine being, and is therefore under
some kind of obligation to follow the instructions of this deity,
then the norm of conduct will be different. This difference is
further emphasized by the fact that this second position also
holds that this life is only a segment of the total existence of the
individual, and that the individual's status in the future state of
existence is determined to a great extent by his conduct in the
present life. Similar actions may be performed in some particular
situation by the theist and the non-theist even though there are

different motivations for the action. An action chosen by the non-theist on the basis of self-preservation may also well be the right action as determined by the instructions of the deity, however these instructions are obtained. The Christian theist would most likely account for this similarity of action by saying that all human beings, by the very nature of their existence, bear the imprint of the creator and that the non-theist may be able to act as he should by the correct use of his natural faculties even without recognizing the existence of God. But the England of Butler's time did recognize the existence of God; so there was no reason for his handling this particular problem.

This general belief in the existence of God by the ethical writers of Butler's day can readily be seen from the brief summaries of their writings presented below. Ralph Cudworth and Henry More are included as representatives of the Cambridge Platonists, John Locke and Richard Cumberland as representatives of the natural law moralists, Samuel Clarke and William Wollaston as representatives of the rationalists, and Anthony Cooper (Third Earl of Shaftesbury) and Francis Hutcheson as representatives of the moral sense approach to ethics. In addition to indicating that Butler's assumption of the existence of God was a comon idea of his day, the sketches of the above men will serve the important function of providing a general background of the thinking of his predecessors and contemporaries against which Butler's own development may be placed. All of these men are ethical theorists and as such maintain that there is such a thing as normative ethics, although they may not agree on what the norm is or how it may be known.

Before summarizing the ethical and theological thought of the age, as these disciplines were the most closely associated with Butler, a short biography will be given. Although he lived the normal, rather uneventful life of a prominent churchman and as such presents little information to be recorded, an attempt to understand the man and how he lived may aid in an adequate interpretation of Butler. The summary of his relationship to theological discussion will also of necessity be brief, inasmuch as little has been recorded of his activities in this discipline. The most important contribution in this section on theology will be the summary of the deistic position since Butler's *Analogy* was written as an apologetic for Christian theism against the natural religion of the deists.

Thus, this study will proceed according to the method of properly interpreting a philosopher mentioned above. After Butler's life and times have been investigated, a sympathetic but systematic study of his writings will be undertaken. Since the *Analogy* gives the most complete discussion of his theistic *Weltanschauung*, it will be discussed first. The *Sermons* will then be analyzed for their contribution to his ethical thought. It is anticipated that this study will indicate that Butler was a thorough theist and that his ethics are harmonious with the rest of his system.

II

BUTLER AS AN INDIVIDUAL

Joseph Butler was born May 18, 1692 at Wantage, in Berkshire, the youngest of eight children of Thomas Butler, a retired linen and woolen draper of substantial means and a respectable reputation. After attending the free grammar school in his home town, Butler was sent to a dissenting academy at Gloucester to study for the Presbyterian ministry. The academy moved to Tewkesbury, and it was from here that in 1713, at the age of twenty-one, Butler began his correspondence with Samuel Clarke by questioning the conclusiveness of a proposition in *A Demonstration of the Being and Attributes of God*. Clarke was so impressed by this exchange of letters, that they were appended to the subsequent editions of this book. Something more of Butler's early interest can be noted in the fourth letter that contains this interesting statement: "For, as I design the search after truth as the business of my life, I shall not be ashamed to learn from any person."[1]

During this time, Butler came to the conviction that he should conform to the Established Church rather than become a dissenting minister. After his father was convinced that he could not be swayed from this decision, Butler entered Oriel College of Oxford University in 1714. There is no record available concerning his ordination nor of the ordaining bishop, but this ceremony probably took place shortly after Butler entered Oxford. In 1718 on the recommendation of Mr. Edward Talbot and Dr. Samuel Clarke, he was appointed Preacher at the Rolls, where he continued until 1726, the year the *Sermons* was published.

[1] I, "Correspondence with Clarke", Letter 4, p. 430.

In 1722 he was appointed Rector of Haughton and in 1725 Rector of Stanhope. While jointly serving the Rolls Chapel and Haughton and then Stanhope, he divided his time equally between his duty in town and in the country, and after he left Rolls Chapel, he lived at Stanhope for seven years. In 1733 Butler was brought out of his rural retirement at Stanhope with an appointment as chaplain to the Lord Chancellor, Mr. Charles Talbot. On his way to London, he stopped by Oxford to receive a Doctor of Law degree, having received his Bachelor of Law in 1721 while at the Rolls Chapel.

In 1736 he was appointed Clerk of the Closet to Queen Caroline and to the Prebendary of Rochester, and in the same year the *Analogy* was published. His special duty as Clerk of the Closet was to be in the Queen's presence every evening from seven until nine in order that he might participate in learned discussions. The Queen died the next year in 1737, but she had so highly recommended Butler to the King, that he was made Bishop of Bristol in 1738. In 1740 he was promoted to the Deanery of St. Paul in London, and because of this appointment resigned the rectorship of Stanhope. A few years later in 1746 he was made Clerk of the Closet to the King, and in 1750 became Bishop of Durham. He had only been in the new See a short time before his health began to decline. He first tried the waters at Bristol and then Bath; but they were both ineffectual, and he died and was buried in the Cathedral at Bristol.

Bishop Butler was reported to have had a retiring and pleasant personality. He was not a dynamic conversationalist nor adept at verbal argument, and because of this, he refused encounters that would lead to such situations. However, he evidently had sufficient ability along these lines to please the Queen. When he first started out in the ministry, he received some financial help from his father, which indicates that they remained on good terms, even though Butler had joined the Established Church. Even when his income increased by his promotions within the Church, he retained a very simple style of living, and spent his money on charity and improving the buildings in his charges. Through his ability and with the help of influential friends, he maintained a steady rate of advancement in the Church until appointment as a bishop. There is a story, which generally is not considered authentic, that in 1747 he was offered the arch-bishopric of Canterbury, but refused by saying something to the effect that it was too late for him to try to support a falling church. As Butler had devoted his life to the Church, this would be a strange reason for declining its highest position.

J. H. Bernard in his edition of Butler's works includes this description of Butler's appearance in 1751.

He was of a most reverend aspect; his face thin and pale; but there was a divine placidness in his countenance, which inspired veneration, and expressed the most benevolent mind. His white hair hung peace-fully on his shoulders, and his whole figure was patriarchal.[2]

During the debate on the Regency Bill also in the year 1751, Horace Walpole made this remark: "The Bishop of Durham has been wafted to that See in a cloud of metaphysics and remained absorbed in it."[3]

Although this introductory study is concerned with the ethical thinkers of the philosophers of Butler's day, a few remarks will be given here regarding two important English philosophers who are not particularly known for their ethical thought but who had some personal contact with Butler. The first one is Berkeley, who is naturally remembered as an another churchman-philoso-pher of the first half of the eighteenth century. Although Bartlett in his biography of Butler devotes an entire chapter to Berkeley, it seems that Butler was never more than a casual friend of Berkeley, and they had little, if any, influence on each other's intellectual pursuits. That they had considerable personal contact is obvious from the fact that Berkeley attended the evening discussion groups held by Queen Caroline when Butler was Clerk of the Closet. Even though it is not possible to know what exactly was discussed at these meetings, Bartlett makes these general remarks.

---

[2] *The Works of Bishop Butler,* Ed. by J. H. Bernard (London: Macmillan & Co., Ltd., 1900), I, xvii.
[3] *Ibid.*

Amongst the distinguished divines, who were often times summoned on these occasions, were, Berkeley, Clarke, Hoadley, Sherlock, and Secker. Berkeley and Clarke were opposed to each other upon their respective metaphysical theories; and, during the discussion of the points of difference between them, Hoadley invariably supported the views of the latter, while Sherlock was rather disposed to favour the speculations of the former. In the absence of evidence upon the subject, it is not difficult to conceive that Butler, although younger than the leading combatants, might occasionally act as *moderator,* and be inclined to repress the excursive flights of the imaginative Berkeley, by adducing arguments more in accordance with the general theory of Dr. Clarke.[4]

During his illness, Butler no doubt tried the tar water remedy so highly recommended by Berkeley; but it evidently was not beneficial in his case.

The other philosopher to be mentioned here is Hume. Although there is no record of Hume and Butler ever meeting, Hume made a decided effort to have Butler read the manuscript of his *Treatise of Human Nature* before it was published. Mr. Home gave Hume a letter of introduction to Butler, but when Hume called on Butler sometime in 1738, he was not at home. The following is taken from a letter of December 2, 1737, Hume wrote to Henry Home, who later became Lord Kames.

Your thoughts and mine agree with respect to Dr. Butler, and I would be glad to be introduced to him. I am at present castrating my work, that is, cutting off its noble parts; that is, endeavoring it shall give as little offence as possible, before which, I could not pretend to put it into the Doctor's hands. This is a piece of cowardice for which I blame myself, though I believe none of my friends will blame me. But I was resolved not to be an enthusiast in philosophy while I was blaming other enthusiasms.[5]

On February 13, 1739, Hume again wrote his friend that he had sent a copy of the *Treatise* to Butler, but had received no reply from him. Hume mentions Butler in the introduction to the *Treatise* along with Locke, Shaftesbury, Mandeville, and

---

[4] Thomas Bartlett, *Memoirs of the Life, Character, and Writings of Joseph Butler* (London: John W. Parker, 1839), p. 41.

[5] *New Letters of David Hume,* Ed. by Raymond Klibansky and Ernst C. Mossner (Oxford: At the Clarendon Press, 1954), p. 1.

Hutcheson as late philosophers in England, who have put the science of man on a new footing. This is of course Hume's avowed purpose as explained in the sub-title, "an attempt to introduce the experimental method of reasoning into moral subjects".

On June 13, 1742, shortly after publishing *Essays Moral and Political,* Hume again wrote to his friend. The following excerpt indicates that Hume was still interested in the reaction of Bishop Butler to his writings.

The *Essays* are all sold in London as I am informed by two letters from English gentlemen of my acquaintance. There is a demand for them ... I am also told that Dr. Butler has everywhere recommended them, so that I hope they will have some success. They may prove like dung with marl and bring forward the rest of my philosophy which is of a more durable thought of a harder and more stubborn nature.[6]

These few remarks are sufficient to indicate that Butler lived the active life of a high ranking churchman. A few more insights will be gained into his character in the next chapter which discusses the theological thought of his day.

---

[6] *Ibid.,* p. 10.

BUTLER AND HIS THEOLOGICAL AGE

It seems rather surprising that for a man who gained as high a position in the Established Church of England, who was prominently in royal favor, and who had so many influential friends as Butler, so little should be recorded concerning his theological opinions. A few of the instances in which Butler's opinion on a theological matter will illuminate his thought will be noted here. Perhaps this deficiency is due to the fact that Butler thought it would be to his advantage to remain publically above the controversies of his age, that he was of a retiring personality, or that he did not have a biographer until several generations after his death. One exception is his strong opinion on deism, and this will be discussed in some detail later.

Although discussion concerning the relationship of church and state was not particularly prominent during Butler's time, he probably would have been classified with those who did not want to see the position of the church violated in any respect with regard to her civil rights. This classification is based on his reluctance to be transferred from the See of Bristol to the See of Durham, since he was aware that the honors of the See were to be violated during his incumbency.

There were difficulties, however, in the proposed arrangement which alarmed the scrupulous mind of Butler, and for a time rendered it doubtful whether he would accept the distinguished mark of favour which his Majesty was anxious to show him. One of these difficulties is then stated by the Lord Bishop of Exeter, upon the authority of Mr. Emm, who was secretary to Bishop Barrington, after having in early life, acted as under-secretary to Butler: 'Bishop Butler, as might be presumed had not sought a translation to Durham; he was purely

passive in it, and not absolutely passive. For, on his privately understanding that it was the intention of the Minister, the Duke of New-
castle, to confer the lord lieutenance, which had hitherto gone with
the Palatine See, on the Lord Barnard, Butler gave it to be understood, that he had not the slightest wish to move to Durham, and was
content to stay where he was; but he would not consent to the See of
Durham losing a single honour, which it had been accustomed to
enjoy, on occasion of his succeeding to it. The lord lieutenance,
therefore, inappropriate as it might be justly deemed, to the mitre
even of Durham, was not withdrawn from it, till the next vacancy.'[1]

In this same general area of ecclesiastical authority, attempts
have been made to draw Butler into the Bangorian controversy
by attributing to him the authorship of "A Letter of Thanks
from a Young Clergyman, to the Rev. Dr. Hare, Dean of Wor-
cester, for His Visitation Sermon, at Putney". Both the external
and interval evidence for attributing this pamphlet to Butler are
inconclusive, although it is attributed to him in a catalog of works
on the Bangorian controversy published in 1761. This particular
phase of controversy between the high and low church parties
was occasioned by a sermon preached in 1717 by Dr. Hoadley,
Bishop of Bangor, "On the Nature of the Kingdom or Church
of Christ". The Bishop attempted to show that the kingdom of
Christ was a spiritual kingdom and that his church was intended
by its Divine Founder, neither to be supported by political favor,
nor impeded by political power.

On at least two occasions, Butler had a personal meeting with
John Wesley, who was one of the best known religious leaders
of the middle of the eighteenth century. Wesley had been preaching without special commission to miners out in an open field,
as was his custom, at Kingswood near Bristol, and Butler as
Bishop of Bristol was investigating the matter. He interviewed
Wesley on August 16 and 18, 1739, and part of the conversation
of the eighteenth was recorded by Wesley in his Journal; but it
seems that Butler made no record of the meeting. Butler, in
protesting the practices of the Societies of Methodists, is quoted
by Wesley as saying, "Sir, the pretending to extraordinary revelations and gifts of the Holy Ghost is a horrid thing, a very

[1] Bartlett, *op. cit.,* pp. 112-3.

horrid thing!" [2] After listening to Wesley explain how he prayed over people who had fits during his preaching, Butler explained.

Very extraordinary indeed! Well, Sir, since you ask my advise, I will give it to you very freely. You have no business here. You are not commissioned to preach in this diocese. Therefore, I advise you to go hence.[3]

A repeated criticism of Butler is that his works as well as this incident exhibit a deficiency of evangelic emphasis. One answer to this criticism is that the prevailing tendency of the age was unfavorable to any but a rational presentation of Christianity within the groups to whom Butler was the minister. Another answer is that Butler's writings were not of a nature to emphasize the gospel. Bartlett meets this objection by noting that only a few of the many sermons that Butler preached are preserved, and from these few it can be shown that Butler held to the essentials of Christianity, although he did not emphasize them.

That he took a correct and Scriptural view of the essential verities of our holy faith, may be clearly collected from his writings; in which he refers to the fall and corruption of man, – to the recovery of the sinner through the great atonement of Christ, – to the necessity of repentance, and faith, and the renovating, and sanctifying influence of the Holy Spirit, – and to a consistent and obedient walk and conversating, as the only safe and satisfactory evidence of the sincerity of the Christian profession. That these great topics are not so prominently exhibited in the sermons alluded, as many might desire them to have been, cannot be denied.[4]

Butler's good friend Samuel Clarke was prominently engaged in the Trinitarian controversy as a reviver of Arianism by his publication of the *Scriptural Doctrine of the Trinity*. The idea expressed is that "the Father alone is the one supreme God; the Son is a Divine being as far as divinity is communicable by this supreme God; the Holy Ghost is inferior both to the Father and the Son, not in order only, but in dominion and authority. Only

  [2] Gladstone, *op. cit.*, II, 434.
  [3] *Ibid.*, p. 435.
  [4] Bartlett, *op. cit.*, p. 281.

Dr. Clarke expresses himself more guardedly".[5] Butler was not active in the controversy, although it should be noted that in the second part of the *Analogy* the indication is that he held to the traditional view.

Shortly after Butler was appointed Bishop of Durham in 1750, he delivered a charge to the clergy in the early part of 1751. Following its publication the same year, an anonymous pamphlet appeared, "A Serious Inquiry into the Use and Importance of External Religion; occasioned by some Passages in the Right Rev. the Lord Bishop of Durham's Charge to the Clergy of that Diocese; – Humbly addressed to his Lordship". This is "the only one of his publications which ever produced him a direct antagonist",[6] and on the basis of certain passages in the Charge, Butler was said to be "inclined to popery".[7]

Butler opens the sermon by lamenting the general decay of religion in England and the fact that religion is losing its influence over men. Among the ways suggested to increase the effectiveness of religion is that of "instructing the people in the importance of external religion", and this is the suggestion which led to the difficulty.

Nor does the want of religion in the generality of the common people appear owing to a speculative disbelief or denial of it, but chiefly to thoughtlessness and the common temptations of life. Your chief business therefore is to endeavour to beget a practical sense of it upon their hearts, as what they acknowledge their belief of, and profess they ought to conform themselves to. And this is to be done by keeping up, as we are able, the form and face of religion with decency and reverence, and in such a degree as to bring the thought of religion often to their minds.[8]

Reference is then given to forms observed in heathen religions as well as in Roman Catholic countries, and this reference to

[5] Charles J. Abbey and John H. Overton, *The English Church in the Eighteenth Century*, Revised and Abridged (London: Longmans, Green & Co., 1896), 204-5.

[6] Joseph Butler, *Works*, ed. by Samuel Halifax (New York: Robert Carter, 1846), xlv.

[7] *Ibid.*, p. ix.

[8] II, "Charge to the Clergy of the Diocese of Durham", p. 405, para. 12.

heathen religions brought on him the additional charge of being "addicted to superstition"[9] as well as being interested in Roman Catholicism. To support his contention of the importance of external religion, Butler refers to the law of Moses in the Old Testament.

So it is obvious how much the constitution of that law was adapted to effect it, and keep religion ever in view. And without somewhat of this nature, piety will grow landguid even among the better sort of men; and the worst will go on quietly in an abandoned course, with fewer interruptions from within than they would have, were religious reflections forced oftener upon their minds, and consequently with less probability of their amendment.

Indeed in most ages of the church, the care of reasonable men has been, as there has been for the most part occasion, to draw the people off from laying too great weight upon external things; upon formal acts of piety. But the state of matters is quite changed now with us. These things are neglected to a degree, which is, and cannot but be attended with a decay of all that is good. It is highly seasonable now to instruct the people in the importance of external religion.[10]

The sermon continues on in the same manner, but enough has been quoted to give an illustration of the material which it contains.

Another factor in this controversy is the fact that, while Butler was the Bishop of Bristol, he erected a marble cross in the chapel of his episcopal house. After his death, another attack began in 1767 in an anonymous pamphlet "The Root of Protest Errors Examined", which stated that Butler died in communion with the Roman Catholic Church. Bishop Secker, a long and close friend of Butler, defended him against this attack. However, the charges do not seem to bear much weight when considered in relationship to the remarks made at various times on Roman Catholicism, although he never discusses the subject as such. A few of the strongest denunciations from the public sermons will be given.

And though that perfection of justice cannot in any sort take place in this world, even under the very best governments; yet under the worst, men have been enabled to lead much more quiet and peaceable lives,

---

[9] Halifax, *op. cit.*, p. xiii.

[10] II, "Charge to the Clergy of the Diocese of Durham", p. 407, para. 15-6.

as well as attend to and keep up a sense of religion much more, than they could possibly have done without any government at all. But a free Christian government is adapted to answer these purposes in a higher degree, in proportion to its just liberty, and the purity of its religious establishment. And as we enjoy these advantages, civil and religious, in a very eminent degree, under a good prince, and those he had placed in authority over us, we are eminently obligated to offer up supplications, and thanksgivings in their behalf.

It is to be remarked further, that the value of any particular religious establishment is not to be estimated merely by what it is in itself, but also by what it is in comparison with those of other nations ... the value of our own ought to be very heightened in our esteem, by considering what it is security from; I mean that great corruption of Christianity, popery, which is ever hard at work to bring us again under its yoke. Whoever will consider that popish claims, to the disposal of the whole earth, as of divine right, to dispense with the most sacred engagements, the claims to supreme absolute authority in religion... [to] consider popery as it is professed at Rome, may see, that it is manifest, open usurpation of all human and divine authority.

Thus corruptions of the grossest sort have been in vogue, for many generations, in parts many of Christendom; and are so still, even when popery obtains in its least absurd form.[11]

Although little is known concerning Butler and his theological age on most questions, his participation in one controversy has established his name in theological history. The deistical controversy was the occasion for the writing of his best known book, *The Analogy of Religion Natural and Revealed to the Constitution and Course of Nature.* It is difficult to give a precise definition of deism, since the name refers to many independent writers of the first half of the eighteenth century who were interested in natural religion. To further cloud the issue, the name "deist" was applied by opponents as an epithet of derision to many who generally would not be classified as deists. However, since Butler's *Analogy* is usually considered an apologetic against deism, some identifying characteristics of this approach to religion will be made.

Christianity traditionally holds that there are two types of divine revelation given to man: special revelation, the writings

---

[11] II, Public Sermon V, pp. 366-7, para. 8-9.

codified into the Old and New Testaments and in some instances various inter-testament writings, and natural revelation, which includes any revelation other than special revelation. In the first half of the eighteenth century all revelation was often reduced strictly to natural revelation, which was accessible to each individual by the proper use of his reason. During the Enlightenment, men were captivated by the possibilities of human reason; this optimistic conception of reasoning ability extended to religion in that man was held to be able to discover his religious obligations by the proper use of his natural reason. The deists maintained the natural revelation of traditional Christianity, but denied the validity and need for special revelation. God had created the universe and had set it in motion, but since then, He has not interfered with the process of natural law instituted at the time of creation. George Galloway gives a good summary of this position.

Natural religion meant belief in a God who existed above and apart from the world. He ruled the world as a moral Governor, and the natural order was his order. It was an order in which virtue was rewarded and vice punished. Christian doctrines like the Trinity, the Incarnation, and the Atonement were dismissed as irrational superstitions, and some of the Deists would have said the same of miracles and retribution in future life. The net result was that natural religion was exalted to be the norm and standard, and Christianity was only true in so far as it republished the elementary truths of natural religion.[12]

The whole tendency of the age was to treat religion as simply a matter of intellectual concern. In fact, some hold that "the great deficiency of the age – a want of spiritual earnestness, an exclusive regard to the intellectual, to the ignoring of the emotional element of our nature – nowhere appears more glaringly than in the Deistical and anti-Deistical literature".[13] This intelllectual emphasis soon led to the religious emotional reactions of the Wesleyan movement. In addition to the rationalistic tendencies of the age, a misuse of special revelation by various factions strengthened the deistic objections to traditional Christianity.

---

[12] George Galloway, *Faith and Reason in Religion* (New York: Charles Scribner's Sons, 1928), 190.
[13] Abbey and Overton, *op. cit.*, p. 93.

The Scripture had for many years been used to sanction the most diametrically opposite views. They had been the watchword of each party in turn whose extravagances had been the cause of all the disaster and errors of several generations. Romanists had quoted them when they condemned Protestants to the stake, Protestants when they condemned Jesuits to the block. The Roundhead had founded his wild reign of fanaticism on their authority. The Cavalier had tests ready at hand to sanction the most unconstitutional measures. 'The right divine of kings to govern wrong' had been grounded on Scriptural authority. All the strange vagaries in which the seventeenth century had been so fruitful claimed the voice of Scripture in their favor.[14]

A list of the important deistic writers would include Lord Herbert of Cherbury, Blount, Toland, Collins, Tindal, and Chubb. Until Tindal wrote *Christianity as Old as the Creation: or, the Gospel a Republication of the Religion of Nature* in 1730, deism had been largely critical and destructive of traditional Christianity. The deists had criticized the mysteries of Christianity, in the sense of holding that revelation could not be contrary to nor above reason; the clergy as corrupting religious worship, and limitations on the freedom of thought imposed by the acceptance of a special revelation; the Scriptures themselves especially in the areas of prophecy and miracles; and the system of rewards and punishments. Tindal went beyond this by giving the deistic substitute for the popular conception of Christianity. A brief summary of his position would include at least the following points.

Tindal's principal position seems to be that God has so plainly revealed himself to each individual man that there is no real need for any other kind of revelation. Not only at particular times and particular places, but under all conditions, God has given to man sufficient internal means of knowing just what it is that God requires of man. In the religion of nature man ascertains his duty by rationally considering the nature of God and the nature of man as well as man's relationship to God and man's relationship to other men. The perfection and happiness of mankind consists in his living up to these duties rationally ascertained. This internal religion of nature is an absolutely perfect religion and any ex-

14 *Ibid.,* p. 78.

ternal revelation can neither add nor take away from its perfection. On the basis of the assumption that human happiness is the ultimate design and end of revelation, all revelations must prescribe the same thing. To suppose that mere positive commands are to be made the ingredients of religion is inconsistent both with the good of mankind as well as the honor of God. God does not act arbitrarily nor interpose unnecessarily. but leaves man to his own discretion. Man as a free moral agent is able to obey reason, natural religion, or God, which three are really the same.

Butler's *Analogy* was published in 1736 when Tindal's book was at the height of its popularity. Mossner,[15] following a widely held interpretation, states that "Tindal's work is rendered doubly important . . . as it is the last great Deistic challenge coming before Butler and the one that he undoubtedly bore in mind more than any other".[16]

---

[15] Ernest C. Mossner, *Bishop Butler and the Age of Reason* (New York: Macmillan Co., 1936), pp. 74-5.

[16] It is interesting to note that Leland's *A View of Deistical Writers*, which first appeared in 1754, does not mention Butler as an anti-deistical writer. It is generally thought that he was too close to the actual situation to make a proper evaluation of all the literature.

IV

BUTLER AND EIGHTEENTH CENTURY
ENGLISH ETHICAL THOUGHT

A. INTRODUCTION

Hobbes' ethical theory had stimulated the England of Butler's day into a fruitful period of study because a number of ethical theorists were opposing the arbitrariness which they found in Hobbes' thought. The approaches used by the different writers can be classified into a few general positions, although there were many writers active during this time. The individuals selected for inclusion in this survey were restricted to those generally considered the more important writers of the main positions. The Cambridge Platonists will be represented by Cudworth and More, the natural law moralists by Locke and Cumberland, the rationalists by Clarke and Wollaston, and the moral sense school by Shaftesbury and Hutcheson.

Butler defies classification within these four positions, although he has often been included with the moral sense approach. There are tendencies in his writings that would relate him to each one of them, but the purpose of this dissertation is not to enumerate the historical relationship of Butler with other ethical thinkers. The reason for including a survey of the ethical thought is to provide the general ethical background for Butler's ethics so that his approach may be better understood. An example of how this will help to understand Butler or some feature of his thought is his assumption of the existence of God at the beginning of the *Analogy*. That this was a point of general agreement in Butler's day and therefore not an unusual assumption to make will be noted from the fact that the writers to be discussed below all include some place in their system for the functioning of deity.

Thomas Hobbes (1588-1679) is to be given credit for precipitating much of the ethical discussion of England in the eighteenth century. Most of the ethical writers were disturbed by their understanding of Hobbes as establishing ethics on a very arbitrary basis, and were interested in constructing a system of ethics on a more sure foundation. According to Hobbes, each individual man possesses the natural right to do anything that he pleases, and his desires are naturally directed either to the preservation of his life or to the securing of heightened pleasure. In his original state, man thus has the right to anything that he is powerful enough to obtain and to retain, which leads to Hobbes' conception of the state of nature as war of all against all.

Thus the theoretical basis of Hobbes' ethical development is egoistic hedonism in that the individual does and should act solely for his own preservation and pleasure. Man, on this interpretation, is not naturally a social creature but is basically selfish, and all the apparently unselfish actions which may be observed are resolved strictly into self-regard. However, man is a rational creature, and, by the use of his reason, man discovers natural laws that are in his interest to obey. These laws can be discovered by the proper use of reason, and they will be observed by anyone who really knows what are his true interests. But, the individual has no guarantee that other people know their true interests and will follow natural law, so the prudent thing to do is to instigate some kind of guarantee.

This guarantee is obtained by the social contract wherein individuals mutually agree to give up certain natural rights. The only way in which this contract can be maintained is for some individual or group to have the power to force everyone to abide by this contract, and for Hobbes this is an absolute sovereign, preferably a monarch. The sovereign who arises out of the social contract retains all of his original rights which are now limited for the other parties in the contract, but he, in turn, is supposed to be guided by the laws of nature. This then becomes the basis of social life, and the final basis of right and wrong for the outward conduct of society are the commands of the sovereign.

The practical basis for determining the rightness or wrongness of a situation depends entirely on positive law directly or on past positive laws which have become social institutions.

While originally Hobbes held that good was anything that satisfied the individual's desires, good has been transformed into that approved by the civil government, since reason informs the individual that the society established by the social contract is the best available means of obtaining satisfaction for his desires. When the individual recognizes that his desires conflict with the desires of other individuals, he naturally wishes to control the actions of others, which is done by means of the social contract. Hobbes seemingly had no quarrel with the recognized social virtues of his day but with the basis on which they were considered valid. In a like manner, the conclusion which Hobbes reached did not disturb the other ethical theorists as much as the reasons he gave for holding them.

It should be kept in mind that the underlying purpose of Hobbes' development was political, since he wished to defend civil authority against the revolutionary strife of England in his day. His theory maintains that civil authority is the basis of social life, and therefore to destroy civil authority would be to destroy social life. His opponents interpreted this development as depriving morality of any objective basis, since right and wrong rest on the arbitrary decisions of the sovereign. Hobbes could have met this objection by referring to the fact that the sovereign is to be guided by the natural laws recognized by the proper use of reason, but in history there are few examples of this ideal sovereign. His opponents were also bothered by the fact that he stripped man of any social qualities, and, contrary to Hobbes, they held that man had social as well as egoistic tendencies. The classical refutation of egoistic hedonism is contained in Butler's *Sermons*.

Although Hobbes undoubtedly was the principal cause of the ethical activity in eighteenth century England, since most of the writers were trying to establish ethics on a firmer foundation than the arbitrary command of a sovereign, Bernard de Mandeville (1670-1733) was actually historically closer to Butler and perhaps motivated him to some extent. His writing is perhaps a sophisticated example of Butler's complaint in the advertisement to the *Analogy* that "it is come, I know not how, to be taken for granted, by many persons, that Christianity is not so much as a subject of inquiry; but that it is, now at length, discovered to be fictitious".[1] Butler repeats this complaint several years later in 1751 by opening his "Charge to the Clergy" of Durham with the lament that there is a "general decay of religion in this nation, which is now observed by every one".[2]

In a manner similar to Hobbes and, as noted above, in line with the popular thought of his day as indicated by Butler, Mandeville expressed the viewpoint that moral regulation is not natural to man but is externally imposed upon him. Speaking as a man-of-the-world who has found that all men are fools and hypocrites, "he is convinced that virtue (where it is more than a mere pretense) is purely artificial; but he is not quite certain whether it is a useless trammel of appetites and passions that are advantageous to society, or a device creditable to the politicians who introduced it by playing upon the 'pride and vanity' of the 'silly creature man'!"[3] In fact, Mandeville makes a great deal of pride. Acts which society calls virtuous are not really due to reason, social feeling, or even to a disinterested sense of duty, but are due to the unconscious or at least hidden working of certain vices, particularly that of pride. This thesis that private vices promote public benefit is developed in his *Fable of the Bees.* The story is of a flourishing colony of bees that suddenly reforms overnight into a sober, frugal, and honest community, but the bees find that in the process of transformation they have destroyed initiative and prosperity, deprived the poor and needy of employment, and generally reduced the community to virtuous but stupid and uninteresting poverty. Man (as in the story the bees) needs the threat of evil to overcome his human inertia and to furnish motivation for these accomplishment which separate

---

[1] I, *Analogy,* "Advertisement", p. 1, para. 2.
[2] II, "Charge to the Clergy", p. 397, para. 1.
[3] Henry Sidgwick, *Outlines of the History of Ethics,* 6th Ed. (London: Macmillan & Co., 1954), 191.

civilization from the barbarians. From this economic thesis, Mandeville draws the ethical conclusion that virtue is closely akin to hypocrisy.

Hobbes and Mandeville provide illustrations of thought that caused many eighteenth century Englishmen to begin ethical inquiry. Our interest in the Cambridge Platonists, the natural law moralists, the rationalists, and the moral sense school is the background they provide for Butler's thought. The two individuals from each of these approaches to ethics included in this survey are the ones generally considered to be the most important. The material discussed in connection with each representative is selected on the basis of the purpose of this paper which is the study of the theistic background of Butler's ethics. This survey does not intend to be a detailed study of each individual, since that would require a separate dissertation on each man; it will merely try to show the main thrust that sets each approach apart from the other ethical approaches.

B. THE CAMBRIDGE PLATONISTS

Ralph Cudworth

The first representative of the Cambridge Platonists is Ralph Cudworth (1617-1688). Although he properly belongs to the seventeenth century as far as his dates are concerned, his *A Treatise Concerning Eternal and Immutable Morality*, which of course was written prior to 1688, was not published until 1731. As an epistemological rationalist, he held that sensation gives no knowledge of reality. Sensation is merely the passive apprehension of particular images that are purely subjective and transient in that they exist only for that particular subject only at the particular instant of experience. The true objects of knowledge are universal conceptions in the sense of Platonic Ideas (which of course lends itself to the name of this approach) that can be apprehended only by reason. Since ethical conceptions are universal ideas, they therefore can only be known through the reason and not through sensation. All of these universal ideas exist in God who is considered as the archetypal mind.[4]

Cudworth maintained that moral characteristics such as good and evil are what they are by nature and cannot have their essence changed by the exercise of will either divine or human. Moral characteristics cannot be arbitrarily changed in the same manner that God himself cannot make a body triangular without that body having the nature and properties of a triangle. If this were not the case, a contradiction would result, since a thing would be willed to be what it is not. All things have a particular essence that cannot be arbitrarily changed.

It is true that God or civil power are able to command a thing to be done that previously was not obligatory, but this does not change the nature of the thing itself. The positive commands of God become obligations only because it is in the very nature of things that the positive commands of God are to be obeyed by his creatures. This difference between things that are naturally good and positively good is that the individual's intellect directly obligates him to natural good and only indirectly obligates him to positive good. Things indifferent by their nature come under an absolute good or evil and thus acquire a new relation. For example, to fulfill a promise is absolutely obligated by natural justice. Therefore, if someone makes a promise as a voluntary act to do something that he was not before obligated to do by natural justice, then, because of this voluntary act, that indifferent thing promised becomes something absolutely good, and stands for the present in a new relation to the rational nature of the promiser and becomes for a time a thing that he ought to do. Since it is the intellectual nature that apprehends obligation, it is by reason that the individual is obligated to obey not only God, but also civil power which has lawful authority. If something is commanded to be done by God or by civil power that is not unlawful in itself, this thing that before was indifferent be-

---

[4] Adapted from Ralph Cudworth, *The True Intellectual System of the Universe with a Treatise Concerning Eternal and Immutable Morality*, Trans. by J. Harrison (London: Thomas Tegg, 1845), Vol. III, Book I, Chaps. 2 and 3.

comes for a time by accident obligatory, and is done by the individual not for its own sake, but for the reason that it is obligatory on the basis of natural justice. The actual nature of the indifferent things that become good according to these circumstances does not change but remains indifferent.

Although it be granted that moral good does not depend upon any created will, yet it could be contended that it must depend upon the divine will. If the nature of good does not depend upon the will of God, it would follow that something was independent of God. The only implication which Cudworth allowed is that good is dependent upon some other aspect of God other than his will. The most likely prospect is the divine intellect, which is also superior to the will because of its very nature. It is not possible that there should be any such thing as morality unless there be a God (in the sense of an infinite eternal mind) who is the source of all things.

Although classifying Cudworth as a Platonist predisposes one to categorize his thought, there are passages, such as the one included in this discussion, which seem to indicate that the problem hovers around the faculty or aspect of the divinity that has precedence rather than developing the idea that the divinity conforms to some standard existing in an ideal realm as in Plato. The standard exists within the mind of God. The emphasis in Cudworth is that things and relations are settled and are not arbitrary, and that even God cannot change the essence of a thing once He has called it into being. His opposition to Hobbes centers in rejecting arbitrariness. Although Butler does not discuss the problem within this particular framework, it does not seem that he would have had any quarrel with Cudworth if this theological interpretation is taken.

Henry More

Henry More (1614-1687), the second representative of the Cambridge Platonists, was a voluminous writer, but the following discussion is limited to his *Enchiridion Ethicum*, a textbook on ethics divided into three sections: (1) happiness and virtue in general, (2) the primitive and derivative virtues, and (3) a discussion of free will and the acquiring of virtue. For More, ethics is the art of living well and happily. Happiness is the pleasure that the mind obtains from the sense of virtue and from the consciousness of right action, i.e., done according to the norm of virtue. Virtue, in turn, is considered as an intellectual force of the soul, which so rules over bodily passions that it easily attains that which is absolutely and simply the best. Although virtue is an intellectual power that is to rule over the passions, the passions precede deliberation and choice, and therefore come from nature and ultimately God. The passions are good when followed according to the law of nature.

Man should have no problem in knowing what he should do, for there are axioms of conduct that are so evident that if a man considers them impartialy, he will immediately accept them. More gives a list of twenty-three axioms with the first ones concerning the duties of the individual to himself that tend to prudence, temperance, and fortitude, and the latter ones concerning the individual's duties to other men and to God, which tend to sincerity, justice, gratitude, mercy, and piety.[5]

That man ought to pursue virtue and to flee from vice is clearly manifested by the dictate of conscience. Moreover, that man is obligated to perform all of the duties of virtue is plain from that law of reason that God has implanted in us, for the human intellect (or right reason) is superior, and all the other faculties are by natural right subject to its control. The fact is that the law of virtue and right reason are the same thing, for virtue seeks nothing in any action that is not the best and that is not approved by right reason. Since this law of virtue and right reason is not any positive or arbitrary thing, but of an eternal and immutable nature, we are bound to obey its precepts and directions by an eternal and indissoluble obligation.

This obligation to pursue what man knows to be virtue can be approached from another standpoint. Since man has the feeling

---

[5] Adapted from Henry More, *Enchiridion Ethicum*, English translation of 1690 (New York: Facsimile Text Society, 1930), sec. I, chap. IV.

that he was not born by chance but was created by God, he doubtless belongs to God by right of creation. Because of this unlimited jurisdiction that God has over man, he is bound to do all those things that by divine law he has been required to do. The divine laws are, of course, none other than eternal and unchangeable reason; they never change even as the figure of a triangle or circle never changes.[6] Although More has many facets to his thought, his emphasis on the unchangeable essence of things as well as his personal contact with Cudworth allies him with the Cambridge Platonists.

Although, as noted above, More's idea of happiness is that of the pleasure that the mind obtains from the sense of virtue, the seat of happiness is not in the intellect, but in a special boniform faculty. This boniform faculty is divinely given so as to enable the individual to distinguish not only what is simply and absolutely the best, but to relish it, and to have pleasure in it alone. While groping for concepts suitable to express this faculty, More likens it to the will that moves with an unquestionable thirst and affection toward an object that has been judged to be absolutely the best. Once the will is in possession of this object, it is so swallowed up in satisfaction with it that it cannot be expressed. Due to the nature of the boniform faculty, anyone who acts according to this faculty conforms to the best and divinest thing that is in man, for it is the most elevated and the most divine faculty of the soul. The study and improvement of the boniform faculty is common to all men, since it is not beyond the ability of any man to love God and to love his neighbor.[7]

For More, then, there is a simple and absolute good in all human actions which is to be sought. Although the nature, essence, and the truth of actions are to be judged by the intellect, the relish that accompanies the pursuing of virtue is seated in the boniform faculty. Man is to pursue because he recognizes it by his God-given intellect, and because he realizes that he is a creature created by God and that therefore he should follow the commands of God.

[6] *Ibid.*, sec. III, chap. III.
[7] *Ibid.*, sec. I, chap. II.

Relation to Butler

Although the purpose of this study is not to trace the historical relationship between philosophers, a few general remarks concerning similarities of thought will be noted. It seems that the ethics of this period can be divided into groups: (1) the rational approach including the Cambridge Platonists, the natural law theorists, and the rationalistic approach of Clarke and Wollaston, and (2) the emotional approach (in the sense of feeling) of the moral sense philosophers. Since Cudworth and More preceded the other two rational approaches, the Cambridge Platonists are related to Butler indirectly through them.

The emphasis of the Cambridge Platonists on moral principles that can be apprehended by reason is certainly in harmony with Butler as well as the other rational approaches. Butler would likewise agree that these principles do not change, but he would allow for development by permitting new principles to be added as is the case with special revelation. Butler also makes a distinction of kinds of obligation similar to Cudworth's division between natural good and positive good.

Although More also is a rationalist, his thought was so fruitful that he also contributed to the emotional approach through his conception of the boniform faculty and perhaps indirectly through Shaftesbury to Butler's emphasis on conscience. In addition to this similarity, the hierarchy of faculties as well as the implantation of reason by God may be mentioned.

C. THE NATURAL LAW MORALISTS

John Locke

Starting in 1942, some of Locke's unpublished papers were turned over to Oxford, and in the collection was a notebook dated 1663 which contained his "Essays on the Law of Nature".[8] In

[8] John Locke, *Essays on the Law of Nature,* Ed. by W. von Leyden (Oxford: Clarendon Press, 1954).

his published works, John Locke (1632-1704) gave indication that he held to such a concept, as can be noted from the following excerpt, but nowhere had he discussed the concept in any detail. These essays complement his thought in this area since they contain such a discussion.

For though it would be beside my present purpose to enter here into the particulars of the law of nature, or its measures of punishment, yet is is certain there is such a law, and that, too, as intelligible and plain to a rational creature and a studier of that law as the positive laws of commonwealths, nay, possibly plainer, as much as reason is easier to be understood than the fancies and intricate contrivances of men, following contrary and hidden interests put into words; for so truly are a great part of the municipal laws of countries, which are only so far right as they are founded on the law of nature, by which they are to be regulated and interpreted.[9]

In the first essay, Locke develops his argument for the law of nature, or as he also calls it a rule of morals. That man along with everything else in the universe has fixed laws of operation appropriate to its nature, is evident from reflecting on God (whose existence is assured by the teleological argument), noting the consensus of mankind at every time and in every place, and by heeding man's own conscience. These rules of conduct are the law of nature that "can be described as being the decree of the divine will discernible by the light of nature and indicating what is and what is not in conformity with rational nature, and for this very nature commanding or prohibiting".[10] It is not the dictate of reason, since reason does not establish the law of nature, but rather discovers and interprets it as a law enacted by a superior power and implanted within the heart of man. All of the requisites of a law are found in natural law: (1) it is the decree of a superior will (the formal cause of law), (2) it lays down what is and what is not to be done (the proper function of law), and (3) it binds men, for it contains in itself all that is requisite to create an obligation, i.e., someone who has right and power over us and to whom we owe a duty.

[9] John Locke, *Two Treatises of Government*, Ed. by Thomas I. Cook (New York: Hafner Publishing Co., 1947), Treatise 2, pp. 126-7, para. 12.
[10] *Essays on the Law of Nature, op. cit.*, p. 11.

In the second essay Locke questions whether or not the law of nature can be known by the light of nature and arrives at an affirmative answer. By the light of nature Locke means "nothing else but that there is some sort of truth to the knowledge of which a man can attain by himself and without the help of another, if he makes proper use of the faculties he is endowed with by nature".[11] That man has in some sense made use of this ability is shown by the fact that there is no nation which does not make a distinction between virtue and vice. As one might expect, Locke goes into the question of sources of knowledge, and notes that there are four possible: (1) innate ideas, (2) tradition, (3) sense-experience, and (4) divine revelation. Only the first three are under consideration since they are within the natural endowments of man, and reason is not included, since it is not a source of knowledge although the law of nature is often called "right reason". Reason merely amplifies and refines the elements of knowledge derived from the four sources. Locke rejects innate ideas and tradition as sources of knowledge, and as he has already eliminated divine revelation, he is left with sense-experience as his only source of knowledge. By the combination of sense-experience and reason, Locke in the fourth essay argues that man can know the two presuppositions required for knowledge of a law: (1) a lawmaker, and (2) his revealed will indicating how man is to act. The senses give information of the orderliness of nature, and from this, reason infers God as the creator of the universe and of man. All men can exercise their senses and reason and are therefore able to discover God for themselves. From the belief in God as creator, it is inferred that God created according to a divine purpose which man is obligated to fulfill.

Having established that the law of nature can be known by man, in essay six Locke argues that man is bound by this law of nature. The origin of both legal and natural obligation is derived from someone who has right and power over man and to whom we owe a debt or duty, and man is able to infer that God created man for a purpose. When the will of God is known by the light of reason, it is called the natural law, and when it is known by

[11] *Ibid.*, p. 123.

revelation, it is called positive law. Both are binding on men, and their only difference is the manner in which they are disclosed by God and apprehended by man. The law of nature is universally binding (Essay VII), since it is so rooted in human nature that before the law can be annulled, human nature must be changed. There is harmony between the law of nature and human nature in the eternal order of things, and from this it follows that what is proper for some rational men at one time, must be proper for all at all times. The moral duties arising out of men's nature are as necessary and immutable as the geometric deduction from the nature of a triangle that its three angles are equal to two right angles.

This does not necessarily mean that the law of nature is static. Although the binding force of the law remains constant, changing times and circumstances help to define obedience. "We can sometimes stop acting according to the law, but act against the law we cannot." [12] Four points can be noted in the development of this principle. (1) Some acts, as for instance theft and murder, are absolutely forbidden. (2) Some acts, as for instance reverence for God, affection for one's parents, and love of one's neighbor are always a duty. (3) Some acts, such as outward worship of God and bringing relief to people in trouble are not to be done continuously, but at particular times and under certain conditions. (4) Although a particular action in itself is not commanded, the accompanying circumstances are in some cases. Man is not obligated to talk to his neighbor, but if he does so, he is obligated to speak in a certain manner. Thus, although the binding force of natural law is universal, natural law is not static since the circumstances of life change.

Even though, as has been pointed out above, man discovers and does not create natural law, it is in man's own best interest to follow natural law. "Nothing contributes so much to the general welfare of each and so effectively keeps man's possessions safe and secure as the observance of natural law." [13] Locke does not develop this trend of thought to any great extent in his final

[12] *Ibid.*, p. 193.
[13] *Ibid.*, p. 207.

essay on natural law, but it is alluded to years later in the *Essay Concerning Human Understanding,* published in 1690. In the intervening years, possibly around 1676, Locke became interested in a hedonistic theory of morality, but this did not replace his earlier theory of natural law. As many of the other ethical writers of his age, Locke is trying to synthesize more than one principle in his ethical thought: (1) moral good as conformity of human actions to some rule (natural law), and (2) moral good as a tendency of objects to produce pleasure in the subject, and moral evil as the tendency to produce pain. Since most men are hedonists and do not bother to inquire into the reason of things, God has joined pleasure with virtue. Men do what is good because it brings them pleasure, but by the proper use of his endowed faculties, man can know that this is also good in itself. This concept that pleasure follows the observance of God's law and pain the breach will be stated in Locke's own words.

Hence naturally flows the great variety of opinions concerning moral rules, which are to be found among men, according to the different sorts of happiness they have prospect of, or propose to themselves: which could not be if practical principles were innate, and imprinted in our minds immediately by the hand of God. I grant the existence of God is so many ways manifest, and the obedience we owe him so congruous to the Light of Reason, that a great part of mankind give testimony to the Law of Nature; but yet I think it must be allowed, that several moral rules may receive from mankind a very general approbation, without either knowing or admitting the true ground of morality; which can only be the will and law of God, who sees men in the dark, has in his hand rewards and punishments, and power enough to call to account the proudest offender. For God having, by an inseperable connection, joined virtue and public happiness together; and made the practice thereof necessary to the preservation of society, and visibly beneficial to all with whom the virtuous man has to do; it is no wonder, that every one should, not only allow, but recommend, and magnify those rules to others, from whose observance of them he is sure to reap advantage to himself. He may, out of interest, as well as conviction, cry up that for sacred, which if once trampled on and profaned, he himself cannot be safe nor secure. This, though it takes nothing from the moral and eternal obligation which these rules evidently have; yet it shows that the outward acknowledgment men pay to them in their words, proves not that they are innate principles: nay, it proves not so much, as that men assent to them inwardly in their own minds, as the inviolable rules of their own practice; since we find that self-interest, and the conveniences of this life, make many men own an outward profession and approbation of them, whose actions sufficiently prove, that they very little consider the lawgiver that prescribed these rule, nor the hell he has ordained for the punishment of those that transgress them.[14]

Butler was influenced by Locke's ethical theory that there are natural laws of conduct. However, Butler emphasized to a greater extent that pleasure and pain have been related by God to these natural moral laws. Thus, man has a guide for his conduct; man obtains pleasure when he is acting virtuously.

Richard Cumberland

Richard Cumberland (1632-1718) is the second representative of the natural law moralists. In his main work on ethics, *The Laws of Nature,* he attempts to deduce from the nature of things the essence, kinds, and obligation of the laws of nature, as well as to refute Hobbes' theory of the state of nature and of civil society. Although Cumberland was quite close to Locke in his development of the idea of natural law, he includes other suggestions for ethical theory, most notably his stress on benevolence, which makes him a forerunner of the utilitarians. Until a few years ago he was, of course, the better known of the natural law moralists; but since his writings are not known for their clarity, Locke's development is easier to follow, and was chosen as the main representative of this approach.

For Cumberland there are natural laws of unchangeable truth that direct our voluntary actions in the choice of good and the refusal of evil and that impose upon man an obligation to regulate his external actions, even without civil law. These laws have a real existence and naturaly carry along with them the force of obligation in their direction of human actions inasmuch as they point out what must be done to attain the end which nature has

---

[14] John Locke, *An Essay Concerning Human Understanding,* 16th Ed. (London: No publisher, 1768), pp. 32-3, para. 6.

determined man to pursue. Man can reason to these general propositions by considering both the causes and consequences of his contemplated action. This consideration of the causes on which he is dependent as well as the near and remote consequences must necessarily lead man to consider not only all other men, but also God as the supreme founder and governor of the universe. The kind of human actions that will chiefly promote the common good of all beings can thus be determined by man's reason, and the law of nature is contained in these propositions.[15]

Cumberland finds that the fundamental proposition of reason is that the greatest benevolence of every rational agent towards all other rational agents constitutes the happiest state of everyone in general and of each individual in particular. Benevolence is the necessary prerequisite in order to attain the happiest state of existence to which all men aspire to the extent it is within their power to procure it, and therefore, the common good of all is the supreme law.

The classification of Cumberland as a forerunner of the utilitarians can be seen from his emphasis on benevolence. There is no better way for a man to pursue his own pleasure than to pursue it in connection with that of other human beings. In fact, there is no other way by which the individual can attain his own happiness than in the way that leads to the common happiness of all. The inner peace of life will be lacking unless this is realized, since it is inconsistent for any individual human being to determine to act according to one manner in relation to himself and another manner in relation to others who are of the same human nature.

Relation to Butler

The ethical ideas apprehended by the Cambridge Platonists were considered to be laws of nature by the natural law moralists. In accordance with Locke's epistemological interest, the natural

---

[15] Adapted from Richard Cumberland, *A Treatise of the Laws of Nature,* Trans. by John Maxwell (London: R. Phillips, 1727), chap. I, sec. IV.

laws were not considered innate; man learns of the natural laws by the proper use of his reason. Because of the fact that there are natural laws, Locke is led into theology, since laws presuppose a lawgiver.

Butler seems to have been considerably more under the influence of this approach than is generally seen at first glance. In the same manner that it is possible to ascertain how the natural realm functions by finding natural law in the manner followed by Newton, so it is possible to find how mankind should function by discovering natural laws of conduct. Butler views the universe as an organic whole functioning by laws. Because God is the kind of a being that he is, Butler maintained that He had fixed pleasurable consequences to virtuous actions and disagreeable consequences to vicious actions. In this manner, by pursuing pleasure and turning away from pain, man is able to ascertain how he should act.

Although Butler did not hold that man should act according to utilitarian principles as did Cumberland, it is sometimes said that Butler thought God had so constituted the universe so as to provide the greatest amount of pleasure for the greatest number of men. Butler also agreed that the individual's pleasure could only be attained by consideration of others.

D. THE RATIONAL MORALISTS

Samuel Clarke

Samuel Clarke (1675-1729) is important for the purpose of this study not only because he was the leading exponent of the rationalistic approach to ethics, but also because he was the closest personal friend of Butler among his philosophical contemporaries. As a thorough exponent of rationalism, Clarke held that the principles of morals are as intuitively evident to reason as those of mathematics and that it is as absurd to deny the one as to deny the other. Any empirical evidence to the contrary, such as the conduct of men and nations, no more proves the absence of such moral principles than their ignorance of mathematics would prove the absence of mathematical principles.

Clarke's basic ethical views are found in the first chapter of his *A Discourse Concerning the Unchangeable Relations of Natural Religion,* which was delivered as the Boyle lectures in 1705. His emphasis is on the necessary and eternal relations that things have to each other in much the same manner as the Cambridge Platonists put the emphasis on eternal essences. The relative fitness or unfitness of things to one another is the standard by which God necessarily chooses to act. God's actions are always agreeable to justice, goodness, and truth and, as such, further the welfare of the whole universe. This same standard should also determine human actions so that their consequences will be for the public good. The eternal and necessary fitness of things lays an obligation on man to act in certain ways, and this obligation is separate from any positive command of God, personal advantage or disadvantage, and reward or punishment.[16]

This summary of Clarke's ethical thought will now be expanded and clarified. That there are differences of things and relations to each other is as evident as a mathematical or geometric proposition. In the ethical realm it thus becomes evident that there is a fitness or unfitness of certain manners of behavior of some persons towards others. As an example, it is undeniably more fit that all men should endeavour to promote the universal good than that all men should contrive the ruin and destruction of all. In a like manner it is evidently more fit that men should deal with one another according to the known rules of justice than that man for his own advantage should cheat, defraud, or violate other human beings.

Clarke thought that these observations were so self-evident that nothing but extreme stupidity, moral corruption, or contrariness could possibly make any man entertain the least doubt concerning them. Any ordinary, unbiased man, who had never

---

[16] Adapted from Samuel Clarke, *A Discourse Concerning the Being and Attributes of God, the Obligations of Natural Religion and the Truth and Certainty of the Christian Revelation,* 6th Ed. (London: James Knapton, 1725).

heard that there were philosophers who had attempted to prove that there is no natural and unalterable difference between good and evil, would at the first hearing be as hard to persuade of this fact as if he were asked to believe that any geometer would seriously and in good faith say that a crooked line is as straight as a straight line. Indeed, it would be needless to attempt to establish the eternal difference of good and evil had not certain men, such as Hobbes, asserted that there is no such real difference in the nature of things, but that all obligation of duty to God arises merely from his absolute irresistible power, and all duty towards men merely from positive contract.

In fact, Hobbes' position leads to a contradiction. If there is no difference between good and evil, then in the state of nature any law or its contradiction is equally good, just, and reasonable. It would be equally good or evil for one man to destroy the life of another as it would be to preserve another's life. To prevent this evil of the destruction of mankind, men enter compacts to preserve one another. Now if the destruction of men by each other be such an evil that men should enter into certain compacts to preserve each other, then, before any such compact, it was also unfit and unreasonable in itself that mankind should destroy one another. Anyone who teaches that good and evil depend originally on positive law, either divine or human, will unavoidably run into the same absurdity. For if there is no such thing as good and evil antecedent to all laws, then neither can any one law be better than another, nor any reason be given why any laws should ever be made.

Because of the character of God, he always acts according to the principles of goodness, justice, and truth, and in so acting furthers the welfare of the whole universe. Since God has made man so similar to himself, man should try to act in conformity to these same principles. Clarke maintained that only negligent misunderstanding or willful passion could cause an individual to act contrary to these principles. Because man is free, he may act unreasonably, but he is acting contrary to his duty. The individual who willfully refuses to honor and obey God who has created and has sustained man, is acting as equally absurd as the individual who asserts that the whole is greater than the sum of its parts. When a rational creature does not act reasonably, he is in effect setting up his own will against the nature and fitness of things, and this is the greatest absurdity imaginable.

No thinking individual can avoid giving his assent to the fitness and reasonableness of governing all his actions by right reason, even though he contradicts this in practice. By his reason, man is compelled to acknowledge that there really is such an obligation upon him, even though at the same time he may in practice disregard it. For the judgment of man's own mind concerning the fitness of the thing and that his actions should conform to such a law is his foremost obligation. Whoever acts contrary to his conscience is self-condemned, and the strongest obligation is the one a man cannot break without condemning himself. Although fear of authority and rewards or punishments are expedients for government, they are only secondary obligations. The original obligation is the eternal reason of the thing.

No man deliberately transgresses these principles without secretly reproaching himself. On the other hand, no man obeys them under difficulty without applauding himself. This is what St. Paul means in Romans 2:14-15 when he says that when the Gentiles which have not the law, are a law unto themselves; which show the work of the law written in their hearts, their conscience also bearing witness, and their thought the meanwhile accusing or excusing one another. The truth that the mind of man naturally assents to the eternal law of righteousness is illustrated by the judgment that men pass upon each other's actions. Men may conceal the judgment of their own conscience, but when judging the actions of others, especially when there is no relation to their own interest, they are commonly impartial. From this the conclusion may be drawn that men know the difference between right and wrong.

Thus it appears that man cannot avoid giving his assent to the proposition that mankind should govern all their actions by the standard of right. This assent is a formal obligation upon every man to conform himself to that standard. It is not necessary to deduce all of the duties of morality or natural religion, since all particular duties can be derived from three general principles. (1) The first rule of righteousness is that man should constantly honor, worship, and adore God as the only supreme author, preserver, and governor of all things. This can be put into practice by employing our whole being for his service and glory in encouraging the practice of universal righteousness.

(2) The rule of universal love is that each man should deal with every other man as he could reasonably expect that man to deal with him in like circumstances, and that in general, man, by universal benevolence, should promote the welfare and happiness of all men. Evidence for the first part of this proposition is that whatever an individual judges reasonable for another individual to do to him, by that same judgment he declares what he should do to someone in a like situation. To deny this is the same as if a man should contend that although two and three are equal to five, yet five are not equal to two and three. The obligation to promote general happiness can be deduced from the natural and necessary difference between good and evil. That which is good is fit and reasonable. Since God always does that which is absolutely the best, so every rational creature ought to do all the good that he can to his fellow men. Except in case of corruption by habitual viciousness, the performance of his duty gives man pleasure and satisfaction, and fills his mind with the comfort that he has done the greatest good that he was capable of doing, that he has best answered the ends of his creation, and that he has most closely imitated his Creator. This obligation to benevolence can also be deduced from the nature of man. Next to natural self-love which everyone necessarily has in the first place for himself, there is in all men a certain natural affection for their children and posterity, who have a dependence upon him, and for his near relations and friends. Because the nature of man is such that he cannot live comfortably in independent families, his circle of close relationships ever grows larger, and only the unreasonable lack of mutual charity keeps it from being universal.

(3) Every man should preserve his own being so as to enable him to perform his duty in all instances. Since man is not the

author of his own life, he does not have just power to take it away. Man is also obligated to attend with diligence and contentment to the duties of the particular station or condition of life in which providence has placed him. He should not be discontent because he is not in a superior station, and he should not be so extremely solicitous to change his state in the future that he neglects his present duty.

The law of nature, which is founded in the eternal reason of things, is as absolutely unalterable as mathematical truth. This law of nature is antecedent and independent of the will of God. Holy and good are not holy and good because they are commanded by God, but God commands them because they are holy and good in their nature. The existence of things and the relation that things have to one another depend entirely upon the arbitrary will and good pleasure of God, who can create and destroy as he pleases, but once things are created and as long as God pleases to continue them in existence, their relations as well as the things themselves are absolutely unalterable. Although virtue is not dependent upon reward and vice on punishment but on the nature of things, few would choose to follow virtue if it conflicts with the comforts of life or with life itself. Rewards and punishments are an after consideration that does not alter the nature of things, but which is an additional weight to enforce the practice of what men were before obligated to do by right reason.

God has brought men and things into being with a certain nature, which implies that men and things have certain relations of fitness and unfitness to each other. The fitness of an action can be ascertained by the proper use of reason. When man acts in conformity with the fitness of a thing, he is acting the way that God has determined he should act, and therefore he is acting virtuously. Moral principles are of the same nature as mathematical principles and are available to anyone who will take the trouble to find them. Butler would have no quarrel with any of this summary.

William Wollaston

William Wollaston (1659-1724) is the second representative of the rationalistic approach to ethics. His one book, *The Religion of Nature Delineated,* had an immediate popularity, but it seems that he carried rationalistic ethics to an absurd extreme. He continues the idea that a thing is what it is and not another thing, and when the proper relation is sustained to a thing as it really is, it is as if this relation were true, and if an improper relation is sustained, as if it were false. The problem in interpreting Wollaston is whether he is identifying right action with truth or whether he is saying that in a moral classification right action is analogous to truth in a logical classification. The former is perhaps the more popular interpretation, whereas the latter is perhaps the more charitable interpretation.

His fundamental axiom is "that whoever acts as if things were so, or not so, doth by his act declare that they are so, or not so; as plainly as he could by words, and with more reality".[17] In his example of the horse theft, the man who has stolen the horse and rides away on that horse certainly uses the horse as it should be used, i.e., for riding, but not that particular horse on which he is riding, since that horse is the horse of another man who has not given permission for use of his horse. The horse is not considered in the full sense of being what it is unless the relationship that the horse sustains to his owner is taken into account. The horse thief is using the horse as if it did not belong to his owner, while the actual circumstances of the situation are that the horse does indeed belong to its owner. Thus a contradiction is involved.

In every voluntary infraction of the actual circumstances of the situation the wrongdoer declares that, although God either has caused or has permitted this thing to be as well as the relations that this thing has, I shall not allow them to be so. I will act as if the situation were not so, since the laws of nature are ill-formed and I will not heed them.[18] However, the true and

[17] William Wollaston, *The Religion of Nature Delineated,* 5th Ed. (London: James and John Knapton, 1731), p. 8.
[18] Adapted from *ibid.,* sec. I, chap. IV.

ultimate happiness of a rational being cannot be produced by anything that interfers with truth and denies the nature of things. Anything which contradicts nature and truth opposes the will of the author of nature, and to suppose that an inferior being may make himself happy by opposing the author of nature and the nature of the thing is the absurd supposition that he is more potent than the author of nature. The true happiness of a rational being cannot be inconsistent with reason.[19]

Relation to Butler

The exposition of Butler which is to follow will indicate that Butler has basically a rationalistic approach to ethics. Since Clarke was a personal friend of Butler, the rationalistic tradition was most likely passed on through their mutual friendship. On occasion, Butler even slips into the extreme of posing evil acts as absurd acts similar to Wollaston, but this is not his usual mode of thought.

Butler agrees with Clarke that God acts so as to further the welfare of the whole universe, but emphasizes that this is not the principle on which man should act, although the results of man's actions will further the general good when he is acting virtuously. This is the manner in which God has constituted the universe. Besides this aspect of benevolence within the individual, Clarke, like Butler, recognizes the basic drive of self-love. Although Clarke speaks of man's conscience, he does not emphasize it to the extent Butler does. Butler also uses Roman 2:14-15 in support of his arguments as his text for Sermon II.

E. THE MORAL SENSE SCHOOL

The Third Earl of Shaftesbury

Anthony Ashley Cooper (1671-1713), better known as the Third Earl of Shaftesbury, was instrumental in inaugurating an ap-

[19] *Ibid.*, sec. II, chap. XI.

proach to ethics that emphasized the psychological nature of man. The development of his theory in *An Enquiry Concerning Virtue or Merit* is based on the assumption that every living creature has a private good and interest that nature has compelled him to seek by every possible means. Since there is this interest or good in every creature, there is also an end to which every thing in his constitution must naturally refer. Now good and its opposite ill are always relative to a system. Something may be good in a limited system, but ill when it is related to a larger system, or, of course, vice versa. As an example, if a distempered man is restrained, he is not called good, since he still has his ill purpose, although restrained by fear of punishment or allured by hope of reward. This emphasis on system is a characteristic of Shaftesbury.[20] Good is not an attribute belonging to a thing itself, but is determined through the relationship that the thing maintains to a wider whole or system, and from this emphasis on system, it would be easy to imply that the good of the species is higher than the good of the individual member of that species. Shaftesbury does develop this by noting that goodness or illness in a creature is only that which is natural and that the natural temper of a creature is entirely good only when all of the passions and affections are suited to the good of the species.[21]

So far he has been talking only of goodness, and mere goodness lies within the reach and capacity of all sensible creatures. However, only man can attain virtue, since it arises from the ability of man to reflect on his own actions as well as the actions of others, and to notice if they are worthy and honest.[22] There is individual virtue when man acts in accordance with his naturally good affections, but there is also the higher or social virtue when man acts in accordance with what is best for the system of which he is a part. In order to deserve to be called virtuous, a man

[20] Anthony Earl of Shaftesbury, *Characteristics of Men, Manners, Opinions, Times, etc.,* Vol. I, *An Enquiry Concerning Virtue or Merit,* Ed. by J. M. Robertson (London: Grant Richards, 1900), Bk. I, part II, sec. I - adaptation.

[21] *Ibid.,* Bk. I, part II, sec. II.

[22] *Ibid.,* sec. III.

must have all of his inclinations and affections, his dispositions of mind, suitable to and agreeing with the system in which he is included and of which he constitutes a part. Therefore, virtue is to have one's affections right and complete not only in respect to oneself, but also in respect to society. This of course implies that there is no opposition between public and private virtue. In fact, to be well affected towards one's own interest as well as the public interest is not only consistent, but inseparable.[23] Since the same regularities of affection which promote the individual's own good also promote the good of others, virtue and interest will be found to agree.

Moral virtue springs only from a love of virtue for its own sake and must be independent of any personal hope and fear. Shaftesbury's polemic against basing the motivation to do good actions on rewards and punishments as well as founding good on the authority of God has caused him to be classified with the deists, but his interests were primarily ethical and not theological. Since man is virtuous when he acts naturally, virtue brings along with itself the reason for being virtuous, and man needs no external motivation. Man has a conscience in the sense that he cannot maliciously and intentionally do ill, without being aware at the same time that he deserves ill in return.

Shaftesbury's conception of the moral sense is the doctrine for which he is most widely known. Although the reason plays an important part in obtaining moral knowledge, knowledge alone is not sufficient for moral action, as the motivation must be supplied by a non-rational factor, the sentiment or moral sense. Shaftesbury himself, as well as his commentators, emphasizes the moral sense over the rational aspect, which of course is the reason for his inclusion in the moral sense approach to ethical thought; but as he was historically one of the first in this development in English thought, his ideas are rather hazy. The moral sense is that sensitivity of human nature that apprehends the intrinsic excellence of virtue, just as material objects are apprehended by the usual five senses. The moral sense is so

---

[23] *Ibid.,* Bk. II, part I, sec. I.

constituted that it immediately approves or disapproves moral actions. When this conception of the activity of the moral sense is linked with his idea of the harmony and proportion of virtue, it is easy to understand Shaftesbury's comparison of ethics to aesthetics. The moral sense leads the individual to love virtue just as the sense of beauty leads the individual to love beauty. In fact, virtue is like beauty both in the manner in which the individual becomes aware of it and in itself. This leads to the conclusion that it is the cultivated gentleman who will have an appreciation of virtue just as he has an appreciation of beauty.

Francis Hutcheson

Francis Hutcheson (1694-1746) was influenced by moral sense philosophy through some admirers of Shaftesbury he met in Dublin when he was there heading a Presbyterian academy in the 1720's. Not only in his writing does Hutcheson argue for the existence of such a thing as the moral sense, but also he argues that the virtuous action, which the moral sense approves, is interrelated with benevolence.

The moral sense is that in man which distinguishes an action as either virtuous or vicious. Some actions are immediately recognized as virtuous, and the individual who is making the judgment has pleasure in the contemplation of such actions in others without there being any advantage to the individual. As Hutcheson is in a sense still arguing against Hobbes, he emphasizes that the motivation for approval of virtuous action is not any intention to obtain even this sensible pleasure, much less the future rewards from sanctions of laws, or any other natural good, which may be the consequent of virtuous action, but an entirely different principle of action from interest or self-love, which is benevolence.

From the analogy that he uses, Hutcheson, at times, seems to make the moral sense an inner sense. Just as the author of nature has determined us to receive by our external senses pleasant or disagreeable ideas of objects, according to whether they are useful or harmful to our body, so also, in the same manner, he has given us a moral sense to direct our actions and to give us still nobler pleasures. The moral sense functions so that while we are only intending the good of others, we also at the same time undesignedly promote our own greatest private good. It is not to be imagined under any circumstances that the affirmation of this moral sense, any more than any of the other senses, presupposes innate ideas. Hutcheson only means that the moral sense is a determination of our minds to receive amiable or disagreeable ideas of actions when they happen to occur to our observation antecedent to any expectation of advantage or loss that might result to the individual from them. This is similar to the way in which an individual may be pleased with a regular form, or a harmonious composition, without having any knowledge of the principles involved, or seeing any advantage in that form, or composition, different from the immediate pleasure.[24]

If someone were to examine all of the actions that are counted virtuous and were to inquire into the grounds upon which these actions are approved, it would be found that in the opinion of the person who is approving them they always appear as benevolent, or flowing from a love of other human beings. As stressed above, the approval of an action is not affected by the relationship of the approver to the action in regard to whether or not he is a recipient of any benefit. In this examination, it will be found that nothing will be classified as virtuous where no benevolence can be imagined; in fact, it will be found that even the actions which are in fact exceedingly useful will be devoid of moral beauty, if it is known that they proceed with no kind intention towards others. Yet, on the other hand, an unsuccessful attempt of kindness or of promoting the public good will appear as the most successful if it were motivated by strong benevolence.[25] It should also be noted here that, although a virtuous action is disinterested from the point of view of the person making the judgment, every moral agent may justly consider himself a

---

[24] Frances Hutcheson, *An Inquiry into the Original of our Ideas of Beauty and Virtue* (London: J. Darby, 1725), Treatise II, sec. I, part VIII.
[25] *Ibid.*, sec. III, part I.

part of this rational system so that he may be in part an object of his own benevolence. The facts of the case are such that the preservation of the system requires that every one be innocently solicitous about himself. Hutcheson concludes from this that any action bringing greater evil to the agent than it brings good to others, however it may evidence strong benevolence in the disposition of the agent, must be founded upon a mistaken opinion of the actions tending to public good when there is no such tendency.[26] This leads into the development of virtue as the greatest good for the greatest number with the possibility of calculations to determine virtuous action.

Whether or not an action is to be called virtuous is the decision of the moral sense, which each individual has to some extent. Although all actions that are called virtuous are found to be benevolent, it seems that it is not their benevolent characteristic that makes them virtuous, but the fact that they are pleasing to the moral sense. In the Lockean scheme, Hutcheson's ideas of the moral sense would be ideas of reflection, since they are based on the individual's ideas of the action. As noted above, the moral sense may be mistaken if the action thought to be virtuous actually brings more evil than good. The God-given moral sense of each individual is active in determining whether an action is virtuous and also approves virtuous action once this determination has been settled.

Since such is the case, how is it possible to say that the laws of God are good? By the very fact that men inquire into the justice of laws themselves, both human and divine, it plainly appears that the individual's first ideas of moral good do not depend upon laws. Human laws may be called good because of their conformity to divine laws; but to call the laws of God good or just, if all goodness and justice are constituted by laws somehow revealed to man, is an insignificant tautology similar to saying that God wills what he wills. In order to call the laws of God good or just, it must first be supposed that there is something in actions which is apprehended as absolutely good, and this is benevolence or the tendency toward the public happiness

[26] *Ibid.*, sec. III, part VI.

of rational agents. The moral sense apprehends this excellence, and then the laws of the deity are called good, when they are imagined to be contrived to promote the public good in the most effectual and impartial manner.[27]

Relation to Butler

The obvious similarity between Butler's development of the function of conscience and the moral sense of Shaftesbury and Hutcheson has often caused Butler's inclusion with the moral sense ethical philosophers. In spite of this obvious similarity, as has been mentioned above, it is contended that Butler's basic approach was that of a rationalist. This should become clearer as Butler's thought is developed.

It is very difficult to give a general statement concerning the relationship of Butler and Hutcheson. It is widely thought that Butler had a greater influence on Hutcheson than the reverse relationship.

Butler in a sense gives his own relationship to Shaftesbury, since he is one of the few philosophical contemporaries mentioned by Butler. In the "Preface to the Sermons" Butler notes that Shaftesbury "has shown beyond all contradiction, that virtue is naturally the interest or happiness, and vice the misery, of such a creature as man, placed in the circumstances which we are, in this world",[28] and as such agrees with Shaftesbury. But then Butler goes on to criticize him for not recognizing that there is authority implied in the idea of reflex approbation. Butler, of course, adds this authority in his development of conscience.

F. TRANSITION

The background sketch of the life and times of Bishop Butler has been completed, and the transition is now being made into

---

[27] *Ibid.*, sec. VII, part V.
[28] II, "Preface to the Sermons", pp. 14-5, para. 20.

his works. Although there are no records of any particularly influential event in Butler's life, the biographical sketch gives some idea of his personality. Even though he is not remembered for any of his strictly theological opinions, it was the main philosophical-theological question of his day, deism, which motivated his writing the *Analogy,* which along with his first three sermons is the basis for what recognition he has received.

Butler's age was a time of active ethical thought, and the summary of this phase of his background covered the four most important approaches of his day. Each approach was represented by the two leading writers with the Cambridge Platonists represented by Cudworth and More, the natural law moralists by Locke and Cumberland, the rationalists by Clarke and Wollaston, and the moral sense school by Shaftesbury and Hutcheson. Butler was influenced to some extent by each of these approaches; but since be added a few innovations of his own, it is one of the interesting problems of the history of ethics to determine whether Butler can be correctly classified with any one of the above or if a new classification is needed. The affinities of thought that Butler had with these various approaches will become clearer as his own ethical system is developed.

V

THEISM AND ETHICS IN THE *ANALOGY*

A. INTRODUCTION

A glimpse at the motivation behind Butler's writing of the *Analogy* will be helpful in determining what he was trying to accomplish. Butler interpreted the attitude of his age as that of no longer considering Christianity a subject of inquiry since Christianity had been discovered to be fictitious. Following from this, all people of discernment supposedly agreed that Christianity should be set up as a subject of ridicule in reprisal for having interrupted for such a long time the pleasures of the world. His modest intention in the *Analogy* is to show that "any reasonable man", who thoroughly considers the matter, will find that it is not the case that there is nothing to Christianity.[1]

In the development of this modest proposal Butler discusses the concept of "probability", which for him by its very nature, is concerned with the imperfect kind of information available to human beings. In fact, this concept has no meaning when it is related to an infinite intelligence such as Butler assumes at the basis of the universe, since to it, each thing is discerned absolutely as it is in itself. But for human beings of limited capacities, probability is "the very guide of life".[2] The fact that certitude is not generally available to human beings does not bother Butler, since, however the degree of probability varies from "the highest moral certainty, to the lowest presumption",[3] it is always suffi-

---

[1] I, "Introduction to Analogy" p. 1, para. 2.
[2] *Ibid.*, p. 5, para. 4.
[3] *Ibid.*, p. 3, para. 1.

cient for action. Speaking in our contemporary terms, it could be said that his "moral certainty" is subjective or psychological certitude. Butler at this point is not concerned with the all-knowing infinite intelligence at the base of his system, but he was looking for a guide to human activity. The prudent man is the one who acts on the basis of the available probable information.

From these things it follows, that in questions of difficulty, or such as are thought so, where more satisfactory evidence cannot be had, or is not seen; if the result of examination be, that there appears upon the whole, the lowest presumption on one side, and none on the other, or a greater presumption on one side, though in the lowest degree greater; this determines the question, even in matters of speculation; and in matter of practice, will lay upon us under an absolute and formal obligation, in point of prudence and of interest, to act upon that presumption or low probability, though it be so low as to leave the mind in very great doubt which is the truth. For surely a man is as really bound in prudence to do what upon the whole appears, according to the best of his judgment, to be for his happiness, as what he certainly knows to be so.[4]

This use of "probability" is strictly the commonsense usage to mean that the occurrence of some event or the presence of some quality is supported by evidence, but that this evidence is not sufficient for either subjective or objective certitude, and is therefore open to doubt. The degree of probability varies, but in any case, it is the guide to human action. Butler makes no effort to refine this concept since this commonsense meaning is all that he requires for his purpose; but he does complain that both the concepts of "probability" and "analogy" have not been properly investigated.[5] His purpose is to show that it is probable that analogical reasoning gives true information, i.e., true in the sense that the description accurately describes the event.

Why is this effort made to show that analogical reasoning gives true information? Butler is arguing against the deists who denied a special revelation from God using as one of the reasons for this denial, the difficulties found in the Old Testament and the New Testament. However, the deists generally accepted the con-

---

[4] *Ibid.*, p. 6, para. 5.
[5] *Ibid.*, p. 7, para. 7. . .

cept of a natural governor of the universe. Butler attempts to show, by the use of analogical reasoning, that if God as the natural governor of the universe (jointly agreed by Butler and the deists) is also the author of the special divine revelation contained in the Old Testament and New Testament (denied by the deists but maintained by Butler), then analogous difficulties will probably be found in the natural order of things and in the special revelation.

Hence, namely from analogical reasoning, Origen has with singular sagacity observed, that 'he who believes the scripture to have proceeded from him who is the Author of nature, may well expect to find the same sort of difficulties in it, as are found in the constitution of nature.' And in a like way of reflection it may be added, that he who denies the scripture to have been from God upon account of these difficulties, may, for the very same reason, deny the world to have been formed by him. On the other hand, if there be an analogy or likeness between that system of things and dispensation of Providence, which revelation informs us of, and that system of things and dispensation of Providence which experience together with reason informs us of, i.e., the known course of nature; this is a presumption, that they have both the same author and cause; at least so far as to answer objections against the former's being of God, drawn from any thing which is analogical or similar to what is in the latter, which is acknowledged to be from him; for an Author of nature is here supposed.[6]

When someone is writing a book of such a type as the *Analogy,* the author does not generally point out the problems generated by his method employed in the book. However, Butler does mention his methodological problem in paragraph 8 quoted above, and this needs to be amplified. Butler was trying to convince those who held that there was an intelligent natural governor of the universe who was also its creator that there was also an intelligent moral governor of the universe who was the author of the Old Testament and the New Testament. Those who denied the religious belief in the divine authorship of the Old and New Testaments used, as one of their objections, the difficulties found in these writings. Butler attempts to show that difficulties analo-

[6] *Ibid.,* p. 9, para. 8.

gous to those found in the Old and New Testaments are also found in nature. Since these difficulties found in nature do not exclude a belief in a divine intelligent natural governor of the universe, the analogous difficulties in Scripture should not exclude a belief in a divine intelligent moral author of Scripture, if one is interested in being consistent. Moreover, since these difficulties are analogous, it is probable that the natural governor of the universe is also the author of the Old and New Testaments. If this can be established, then man has two revelations: (1) nature and (2) special revelation in the Old and New Testaments. Just as probability is the guide of life in practical matters, so it should also be the guide of life in religious matters. However, there is a difficulty in this method, and it is conceivable that a different conclusion will follow than the one sought by Butler. An honest inquirer may be so impressed by the difficulties that he finds in the Old and New Testaments that he will be led to exclude the possibility of a divine author (as the deists concluded), and because these difficulties are analogous to those found in the natural order of the universe, one may exclude the possibility of an intelligent natural governor. It is conceivable that the method of analogical reasoning could go both ways.

However, Butler did not have to worry about this second alternative in his immediate situation, since his opponents, the deists, did believe in a divine natural governor of the universe. It is evident that Butler's whole approach rests on this assumption of an intelligent natural governor of the universe. There seems to be no *a priori* reason for denying this to be a legitimate assumption, and, as it has been pointed out in Chapter IV above, it was a common position of his day. But Butler is interested in the positive aspect of this assumption rather than the mere shifting of the burden of proof to ask for reasons why this assumption should not be made.

[The presumption of a natural governor of the universe] has been often proved with accumulated evidence; from this argument of analogy and final causes; from abstract reasonings; from the most ancient tradition and testimony; and from the general consent of mankind. Nor does it appear, so far as I can find, to be denied by the generality of those who profess themselves dissatisfied with the evidence of religion.[7]

A person arguing today would be foolish to start at the same place as Butler did in his argument, since the contemporary intelligensia does not share a belief in a divine natural governor of the universe; but this assumption was meaningful when taken in the context of his age. Butler himself, as may be noted in the above quotation, seems to hold that the traditional arguments for the existence of God are valid, although he worded them somewhat differently than is usually done. Whether or not this belief in the arguments for the existence of God was shared by Butler's contemporaries is unimportant, since the consensus of the intellectual world of his age did accept an intelligent natural governor. In order to gain a hearing today, an apologetic, such as Butler's, would have to argue that any *Weltanschauung* begins with initial assumptions and that the assumptions of theism are as credible as those of any of its competitors. The criteria of choice between the competing assumptions consists of their comparative simplicity, their explanatory fruitfulness, their conformity to available knowledge, plus the subjective reaction of the chooser.

Butler, however, did not appreciate the hypothetical method, since he thought that the tendency would be to speculation which would be unrelated to the facts of experience. Instead of focusing attention on the constitution of the universe as it really is, the speculator will state how the universe should be, and will most likely arrive at two conclusions: all creatures should be made as perfect and happy as possible, and all creatures should be so made that they will always do what is right and most conducive to happiness. If such were the case, there would be no punishment. Butler would agree that "we must conclude the ultimate end designed, in the constitution of nature and conduct of Providence, is the most virtue and happiness possible"; but the individual is not able to know the means by which this could be accomplished in the vastness of the universe in both the spacial and temporal aspects.

---

[7] *Ibid.*, p. 12, para. 10.

Our whole nature leads us to be ascribe all moral perfection to God, and to deny all imperfection of him. And this will for ever be a practical proof of his moral character, to such as will consider what a practical proof is; because it is the voice of God speaking in us. And from hence we conclude, that virtue must be the happiness; and vice the misery, of every creature; and that regularity and order and right cannot but prevail finally in a universe under his government. But we are in no sort judges, what are the necessary means of accomplishing this end.[8]

From this it can be seen why it is said that, for Butler, God was a utilitarian, i.e., God makes the choices which produce the greatest amount of happiness for his creatures. However, it does not follow from this that man should be a utilitarian, since man is not able to know which choice will produce the greatest amount of pleasure. This can only be the activity of an infinite knowledge. In this quotation, Butler states that we know that God is moral because of the voice of God which speaks in us. He does not develop this idea here in the introduction; but this is the same as what in other places he calls conscience,[9] and it is an important concept in his system.

Instead of imagining how the world should be, Butler wants to turn to a study of the conduct of intelligent creatures in the world as it actually is, and the information obtained "may be resolved into general laws or rules of administration, in the same way as many of the laws of nature respecting inanimate matter may be collected from experiments".[10] By using the scientific method of collecting instances upon which generalizations can be based, Butler wants to study the natural order of man's actions. Then he wants to take these generalizations and compare them with the condition of things which religion teaches us to expect with the purpose of showing the analogy between them. "Upon such a comparison it will, I think, be found . . . that both may be traced up to the same general laws, and resolved into the same principles of divine conduct." [11]

---

[8] *Ibid.*, pp. 14-5, para. 13.
[9] See chap. VI below, pp. 140 ff.
[10] I, "Introduction to the Analogy", p. 15, para. 14.
[11] *Ibid.*

In concluding this introduction to the *Analogy* it seems only proper that Butler himself should be quoted concerning his purpose.

[The *Analogy*] will undeniably show . . . that the system of religion, both natural and revealed, considered only as a system, and prior to the proof of it, is not a subject of ridicule, unless that of nature be so too. And it will afford an answer to almost all objections against the system both of natural and revealed religion; though not perhaps an answer in so great a degree, yet in a very considerable degree an answer to the objections against the evidence of it: for objections against a proof, and objections against what is said to be proved, the reader will observe are different things.[12]

B. THE IMMORTALITY OF HUMAN BEINGS

Following this introduction, Butler begins his argument for immortality in the first part of the *Analogy* entitled "Of Natural Religion". He starts at this point since he regards it as "the foundation of all our hopes and of all our fears; all our hopes and fears, which are of any consideration".[13] His pattern of argument is to move from a consideration of the several changes that each individual has already undergone in his life and the changes which lie ahead in the aging process, without the destruction of the individual, to suggest that the change which is called "death" also will not destroy the individual. The charge of false analogy could perhaps be raised at this point because all changes before death, however varied they may be, are connected with a physical body; but, at death, the body ceases to exist. Butler's argument, however, should be analyzed before criticisms are given.

From our being born into the present world in the helpless imperfect state of infancy, and having arrived from thence to mature age, we find it to be a general law of nature in our own species, that the same creatures, the same individuals, should exist in degrees of life and perception, with capacities of action, of enjoyment and suffering, in one period of their being, greatly different from those appointed them in another period of it.[14]

---

[12] *Ibid.*, p. 16, para. 15.
[13] *Ibid.*, p. 18, para. 17.
[14] I, *Analogy,* chap. I, p. 21, para. 2.

Butler continues this argument by appealing to the changes which can be observed in other individual creatures such as insects, birds, and animals. This appeal is of interest because Butler is making use of empirical means to establish the fact of vast changes in the same living creatures with the hope of laying a foundation for a comparison of the change that man undergoes at death to a non-empirical state. He concludes "that we are to exist hereafter [i.e., after death] in a state as different (suppose) from our present, as this is from our former [i.e., human existence in the womb compared to maturity], is but according to the analogy of nature; according to a natural order or appointment of the very same kind, with what we have already experienced".[15]

Butler's argument can be arranged in the form of a hypothetical syllogism.

If an individual remains permanent throughout changes of great degrees of quatity and quality, then it is reasonable to hold that this same individual will remain permanent throughout the future change of death.

By empirical evidence, it can be established that an individual remains permanent throughout changes of great degrees of quantity and quality.

Therefore, it is reasonable to hold that this same individual will remain permanent throughout the future change of death.

Now this poses a problem. Butler in all likelihood does not want to argue for the immortality of insects, birds, and animals, and would prefer to leave this a moot question; but the evidence presented to affirm the antecedent would substantiate this as well as his application to man. He would perhaps attempt to get out of this difficulty (if he would consider it as much) by maintaining either that man is of an essentially different nature than other living creatures, since Butler lived many years before Darwin's theory of biological evolution appeared on the scene, or that this evidence is introduced only to show that changes do occur in nature without the loss of identity and creatures other than man may very well be immortal; we just do not know.[16] The second alternative would escape the charge of false analogy,

---

[15] *Ibid.*, p. 22, para. 3.
[16] The latter is Butler's position in *ibid.*, pp. 37-8, para. 21.

but in either case, the hypothetical syllogism as formulated above would not have to be changed.

Although Butler seems to argue as is outlined above in accordance with his methodological principles in the *Analogy,* perhaps this really is not his method of arguing. All he is really saying is that since man can does survive changes, it is reasonable to think that he will be able to survive the future change of death. But, if we have to make the above concession to creature other than man since Butler introduces this as evidence, it is not strong enough for him to say that we have no reason to think that man does not continue to exist, because his whole development in the remainder of the first part of the *Analogy* hinges on the continued existence of man after death. Implicitly, Butler declares that man is immortal, and then he uses empirical data to establish the fact of individual permanence through vast changes in the order of nature. The change of death is analogous to other changes during the life of the individual, and so it is reasonable to suppose that individual permanence will also remain throughout the change of death. Although it is at times precarious to argue on the meaning of one word, it seems that Butler betrays his position by the use of "appointed" in the last lines of the two above quotations. In the order of nature, the natural governor of the universe has appointed various stages through which each individual passes, and the last earthly stage is death. Death is not the end of the individual, but one stage in the continuing existence of the immortal individual.

This mode of arguing presupposes the uniformity of nature; but for Butler, this is no *ad hoc* assumption, since its basis is in the natural governor of the universe. The terminology used to express this concept is "continuance", "which seems our only natural reason for believing the course of the world will continue tomorrow, as it has done so far as our experience or knowledge of history can carry us back".[17] There is the probability "that all things will continue as they are, in all respects, except those in which we have some reason to think they will be altered".[18]

[17] *Ibid.*, p. 23, para. 4.
[18] *Ibid.*

Butler does not mean to base continuance on man's experience, but this is the way man knows of continuance. Nor does he mean that God is active in a continuous creation; he was too much under the influence of deism to believe this. Since there is no prior reason to the event of death itself to think that the individual's substance changes nor that the "faculties of perception and of action" will be destroyed, there is a high probability that they will continue after death. This idea of "faculties of perception and of action" is not discussed by Butler in any of his writings; it is very difficult, therefore, to know exactly what he meant. He seems to imply that perception and action continue in some manner after the dissolution of the body at the time of death. It would therefore be necessary to attribute to the substance of man, which remains constant throughout all the changes of life, the power of perception and action apart from the physical body in which this substance is embodied prior to the time of death. Almost every theory of personal immortality holds that there is perception in some unspecified sense as well as the possibility of action by man after death.

The word "substance" was introduced into the discussion in the above paragraph; the one sentence where Butler uses it at this stage of his development will be quoted. "It seems [that continuance is] our only reason for believing, that any one substance now existing will continue to exist a moment longer; the self-existent substance only excepted." [19] However, this incidental mention of the word "substance" gives an insight into the framework of Butler's thought. There are two levels of "existence" which can be distinguished in theism: (1) the level of the self-existent substance that obviously is the God of Butler's system, and (2) the level of substances that exist in experience including men and things. It could be implied from Butler's statement and the normal connotation of "substance" that at least to some extent the "substance now existing" is dependent upon "the self-existing substance". As is common to all types of theism, Butler's position is that of philophical idealism. The meaning of "idealism" used in order to make this classification, and which is con-

[19] *Ibid.*

sidered here to be a basic meaning of this term, is that there is another realm or level of existence other than, and more basic than, and of a kind different from, the realm or level of experience. Butler spells out the nature of this other level; it is the theistic God who is the natural as well as the moral governor of the universe.

Since several comments have been made on the fourth paragraph of Chapter One, the important sentences will be given as a unit so that the flow of Butler's thought may be followed.

We know we are endued with capacities of action, of happiness and misery: for we are conscious of acting, or enjoying pleasure and suffering pain. Now that we have these powers and capacities before death, is a presumption that we shall retain them through and after death; indeed a probability of it abundantly sufficient to act upon, unless there be some positive reason to think that death is the destruction of those living powers: because there is in every case a probability, that all things will continue as we experience they are, in all respects, except those in which we have some reason to think they will be altered. This is that *kind* of presumption or probability from analogy, expressed in the very word *continuance,* which seems our only natural reason for believing the course of the world will continue to-morrow, as it has done so far as our experience or knowledge of history can carry us back. Nay, it seems our only reason for believing, that any one substance now existing will continue to exist a moment longer; the self-existent substance only excepted.[20]

As is implicit in all types of personal immortality, Butler has a mind-body dualism. Although the physical body is destroyed at death, which is an empirical fact that cannot be denied, the individual does not cease to exist. Some immaterial aspect of the individual continues to exist; it is an immaterial aspect which continues to exist since the material dissolves. Butler does not go on to spell out the relationship between the mind and body in a human organism as it exists in this life; but it seems reasonable to conclude that the immaterial and immortal aspect would be of primary importance because it can exist in some sense apart from the material aspect and because of the very fact that it is immortal. The manner in which Butler argues is that, since we do not know what death is in itself, but only the effects of

[20] *Ibid.*

death which is the dissolution of the body, we have no reason to think that death is the end of the living agent. In fact, little is known about the functions of the living agent in this life.

And besides, as we are greatly in the dark, upon what the exercise of our living powers ... themselves depend upon; the powers themselves as distinguished, not only from their actual exercise, but also from the present capacity of exercising them; and as opposed to their destruction: for sleep, or however a swoon, shows us, not only that these powers exist when they are not exercised, as the passive power of motion does in inanimate matter; but shows also that they exist, when there is no present capacity of exercising them: or that the capacities of exercising them for the present, as well as the actual exercise of them, may be suspended, and yet the powers themselves remain undestroyed. Since then we know not at all upon what the existence of our living powers depends, this shows further, there can no probability be collected from the reason of the thing, that death will be their destruction: because their existence may depend upon somewhat in no degree affected by death.[21]

This immaterial aspect of man would no doubt be the substance of man that will continue to exist after death; but this immaterial aspect of man is dependent upon the self-existent substance, which is the natural and moral governor of the universe.

In his argument, Butler refers to the substance of man as "the living agent",[22] and takes great pains to show that it is separate from and different from the physical body. He uses the traditional argument that all that can be destroyed is a compound. "But, since consciousness is a single and indivisible power",[23] it cannot be destroyed. Although the consciousness [i.e., the living agent] forms a unity with the body in which it is dwelling, it is not a necessary unity.

It is as easy to conceive, that we may exist out of bodies, as in them; that we might have animated bodies of any other organs and senses wholly different from these now given us, and that we may hereafter animate these same or new bodies variously modified and organized; as to conceive how we can animate such bodies as our present.[24]

After this free expression of the imagination, it almost seems as

[21] *Ibid.*, p. 25, para. 6.
[22] *Ibid.*, p. 29, para. 11 ff.
[23] *Ibid.*, p. 28, para. 10.
[24] *Ibid.*, p. 29, para. 11.

if Butler is ready to argue for transmigration of souls; but his purpose, of course, is to stress the separateness of the living agent from the body in which the living agent happens to be during the present state of existence.

And lastly, the dissolution of all these serveral organized bodies, supposing ourselves to have successively animated them, would have no more conceivable tendency to destroy the living beings ourselves, or deprive us of living faculties, the faculties of perception and of action, than the dissolution of any foreign matter, which we are capable of receiving impressions from, and making use for the common occasions of life.[25]

The other line of approach that Butler uses to substantiate the separateness of the living agent from the physical body is that an individual human being may lose varied parts of his physical body and yet remain the same living agent. Now Butler realizes that characteristics cannot be assigned to the living agent from observation because of the very nature of the thing; but he does want to persuade his reader that because of the possible separation of the living agent from the physical body, there is no reason to believe that the destruction of the physical body is also the destruction of the living agent. Whether or not the two approaches utilized here actually give evidence for the possible separation of the living agent from the body is debatable. However, the fact remains that this separateness is what Butler wishes to establish, and which in effect he must establish to some extent, if his argument based on an appeal to empirical evidence is to be valid.

From these two questionable arguments, Butler goes on to another argument which is definitely contrary to the facts of physics as they are understood today.

That we have no way of determining by experience, what is the certain bulk of the living being each man calls himself; and yet, till it be determined that it is larger in bulk than the solid elementary particles of matter, which there is no ground to think any natural power can dissolve, there is no sort of reason to think death to be the dissolution of it, or the living being, even though it should not be absolutely indiscerptible.[26]

[25] *Ibid.*
[26] *Ibid.*, p. 31, para. 14.

In this argument Butler runs into the difficulty that faces anyone who argues from the science of his particular day – science changes. It may well be the case that certain of his readers may have been persuaded by this argument before the atom was split, but it is no longer of any argumentative force. Butler himself does not use the word "atom", but this seems to be his meaning here, and he is so interpreted by Gladstone. However, the fact that Butler uses poor or even false arguments does not necessarily mean that the conclusion that he was trying to establish is false in the sense that the conclusion as a proposition does not accurately describe an event. The conclusion of a syllogism may happen to be true, although the premises of the syllogism may not be true. This is not an apology for poor argumentation, but merely a reminder to keep a proper historical perspective. After this poor argument, Butler goes on to one, which perhaps has more weight. He notes that "we have several times over lost a great part or perhaps the whole of our body, according to certain common established laws of nature; yet we remain the same living agents: when we shall lose as great a part, or the whole, by another common established law of nature, death; why may we not also remain the same"? [27]

In pursuing this idea that the physical body is no part of the living agent, Butler adds an argument which would give the impression that he could be classified as an interactionist in respect to the mind-body problem. If it is adequate to classify mind-body theories under five heads, three can be eliminated on the basis of what Butler says. Of the five, interactionism, parallelism, epiphenomenalism, panpsychism, and the theory of double aspect, the double-aspect theory is eliminated, since God is self-sufficient substance and man created substance, and therefore different. Epiphenomenalism is dismissed on the basis of Butler's constant insistence of the relative unimportance of the physical body to the living agent; panpsychism is dismissed because, even though the physical body is considered of secondary importance in the total existence of the living agent, nevertheless, it is inorganic. This leaves interactionism and parallelism as possible

[27] *Ibid.*, p. 32, para. 15.

alternatives. Butler does not discuss this problem as such, but the suggestions that can be gleaned from his work favor inter-actionism over parallelism and therefore eliminate the latter. Although the positive evidence for interactionism comes in a rather round-about way, it seems to be conclusive. The sense organs are to be conceived as instruments of perception in much the same manner as sight can be assisted by glasses. "Nor is there any reason to believe, that we see with them [i.e., the eyes] in any other sense; any other, I mean, which would lead us to think the eye itself a percipient." [28] The other senses are like the eyes in the respect that they are instruments of perception and not the perceiver. Butler's whole purpose is to bring in another example of how the living agent is separate from the body and concludes that in dreams the individual is "possessed of a latent, and what would otherwise be, an unimagined unknown power of perceiving sensible objects, in as strong and lively a manner without our external organs of sense as with them".[29] Be that as it may, the sense organs, even in the sense of instruments as Butler conceives them, are the means in the present life to con-vey the object to the perceiving power, which is the living agent. But the possibility of effect of the body on the mind does not end with the reception of sense perceptions. Several paragraphs later, Butler mentions at least one other effect. "Several things indeed greatly affect all our living powers, and at length suspend the exercise of them; as for instance drowsiness, increasing till it ends in sound sleep." [30] This is one side of interactionism with the body affecting the mind, but there is also the possibility of the mind affecting the body.

Thus a man determines, that he will look at such an object through a microscope; or being lame suppose, the he will walk to such a place with a staff a week hence. His eyes and his feet no more determine in these cases, than the microscope and the staff. Nor is there any ground to think they any more put the determination in practice; or that his eyes are the seers or his feet the movers, in any other sense than as the microscope and the staff are. Upon the whole then,

[28] *Ibid.*, p. 34, para. 17.
[29] *Ibid.*, p. 35, para. 18.
[30] *Ibid.*, pp. 40-1, para. 25.

our organs of sense and our limbs are certainly instruments which the living persons ourselves make use of to perceive and move with.[31]

This is interactionism; the body can affect the mind, and the mind can affect the body in which it is dwelling in the present life.

One rather short sentence in Butler's discussion of eye glasses and sense organs as instruments again gives evidence of his theistic framework. "Both [i.e., the glasses and sense organs] are in a like way instruments of our receiving such ideas from external objects, as the Author of nature appointed those external objects to be the occasions of exciting us." [32] Not only is the realm of experience dependent upon the self-existent realm for its very existence, but the Author of nature has so arranged the living agent and the external world apart from the living agent that perception is possible. This description of the universe, which includes both a theistic framework for metaphysics and epistemology, is called theistic realism.

Since the purpose of this study is not to write a commentary on the works of Butler but is an attempt to explicate his theistic framework, the remainder of his discussion in advocating a future life will not be traced. Because of Butler's own admission that a future life is basic to his system, his own conclusion regarding this subject will be given.

But if, as was above intimated, leaving off the delusive custom of substituting imagination in the room of experience, we would confine ourselves to what we do know and understand; if we would argue only from that, and from that form our expectation; it would appear at first sight, that as no probability of living things ever ceasing to be so, can be concluded from the reason of the thing; so none can be collected from the analogy of nature; because we cannot trace any living being beyond death. But as we are conscious that we are endued with capacities of perception and of action, and are living persons; what we are to go upon is, that we shall continue so, till we forsee some accident or event, which will endanger those capacities, or be likely to destroy us: which death does in no wise appear to be.[33]

---

[31] *Ibid.*, pp. 35-6, para. 19.
[32] *Ibid.*, p. 34, para. 17.
[33] *Ibid.*, p. 44, para. 30.

According to Butler's own summary, his argument for a future life rests on the doctrine of continuance with the corollary of the incapacity of death to destroy man. As has been noted above, this doctrine of continuance is Butler's version of the idea of the uniformity of nature. Now this approach was probably cogent in Butler's historical context because both Butler and the deists against whom he was arguing maintained that there was a transcendental God who was the natural governor of the universe. In particular, the deist conception of God is often likened to a perfect watchmaker who was able to construct such a perfect watch that it would never be out of beat nor need any adjustment. So God created the universe and flung it off into space where it continues to function by natural law without any need of outside interference from God. Both Butler and the deists had a metaphysical basis for the uniformity of nature. But Butler, as a theist, would not want to say that God is unconcerned with the affairs of the universe and that God allows it to go on its own course. For him, God, at times, finds that it is necessary to step into the course of things and make necessary adjustments. However, the corollary which Butler draws from this argument does not seem to cary much weight. Since no living being can be traced after death, we have no evidence as to whether or not death ends the existence of a living being. If this argument is approached from the aspect that there is no evidence that death ends existence, it seems to be an argument from silence. If it is combined with the doctrine of continuance, it then seems to be open to the charge of false analogy, since death is different from any other change through which the living being passes, at least in the aspect that the material part of the body, in distinction from the immaterial, is destroyed. Nevertheless, this argument was strong enough for Butler and seemingly for the many readers who kept the *Analogy* widely circulated for over one hundred and fifty years.

Before moving on to the next step in Butler's argument, a few remarks should be made about Dissertation I, "Of Personal Identity". In the first edition of the *Analogy* it was included in chapter one on a future life, but starting with the second edition, it was made an appendix. Butler takes up the question because he thinks some strange ideas have arisen about "the meaning of that identity or sameness of person, which is implied in the notion of our living now and hereafter, or in any two successive moments".[34] Since he is trying to establish the existence of the living agent after death, this problem is of importance to his argument. For Butler, the concept of "personal identity" is a simple concept such as similitude and equality, and "all attempts to define would but perplex it".[35]

For as, upon two triangles being compared or viewed together, there arises to the mind the idea of similitude; or upon twice two and four, the idea of equality; so likewise, upon comparing the consciousnesses of one's self, or one's own existence, in any two moments, there as immediately arises to the mind the idea of personal identity. And as the two former comparisons not only give us the ideas of similitude and equality; but also show us, that two triangles are alike, and twice two and four are equal: so the latter comparison not only gives us the idea of personal identity, but also shows us the identity of ourselves in those two moments; the present, suppose, and that immediately past. Or in other words, by reflecting upon that, which is my self now, and that, which was myself twenty years ago, I discern they are not two, but one and the same self.[36]

Although the comparison of the individual's consciousness of the present with some past time is the basis of the living being ascertaining his personal identity, this is not to say that consciousness makes personal identity. "One should really think it self-evident, that consciousness of personal identity presupposes, and therefore cannot constitute, personal identity; any more than knowledge, in any other case, can constitute truth, which it presupposes." [37] Butler holds that to say consciousness makes personal identity is the same as to say "that a person has not existed a single moment, nor done one action, but what he can remember,[38] and this is ridiculous.

Butler, therefore, wants to say that the living being is imme-

[34] *Ibid.*, p. 387, para. 1.
[35] *Ibid.*, p. 387, para. 2.
[36] *Ibid.*, p. 387-8, para. 2.
[37] *Ibid.*, p. 388, para. 3.
[38] *Ibid.*

diately aware of personal identity upon the comparison of his present consciousness with some past consciousness, and that this is an indefinable concept. Although our present consciousnes of ourselves is necessary for our personal identity now, this does not mean that "present consciousness of past actions or feeling is . . . necessary to our being the same persons who performed those actions or had those feelings".[39] The only thing he is interested in establishing is the continued existence of the personal identity of each human being.

Of the three propositions that have been held in the history of theism, Butler has assumed one, the existence of God, and has argued at length for the second, the immortality of the individual. His next step is to argue that the individual's condition in the future state is dependent to some extent on his actions in the present state of existence.

C. THE GOVERNMENT OF GOD BY REWARDS AND PUNISHMENTS

Because human beings have the capacity for both happiness and misery, the question of a future life is of great importance, especially when the supposition is made that the individual's happiness or misery in the future life is dependent to some extent upon his actions in the present life. If there were no connection between the present life and the future life, Butler thought any speculation about the future life would only be idle curiosity. On the other hand, if the supposition is true that there is a connection, on any ground whatever, however slight, the reasonable man would take care to secure his happiness in the future life. Butler, of course, thinks that there is a connection between the present and the future life, and argues for the reasonableness of this contention.

In our present life, all the pleasures which an individual enjoys and most of the miseries which an individual suffers are within the individual's own power. "Pleasure and pain are the consequences of our actions: and we are endued by the Author of our

[39] *Ibid.*, p. 390, para. 3.

nature with capacities of foreseeing these consequences." [40] The individual has to take care of himself within his human limits, and in the course of life he soon finds that the external things that are the objects of human passions neither can be obtained nor enjoyed without some self-exertion.

I know not, that we have any one kind or degree of enjoyment, but by the means of our own actions. And by prudence and care, we may, for the most part, pass our days in tolerable ease and quiet; or, in the contrary, we may, by rashness, ungoverned passion, wilfulness, or even by negligence, make ourselves as miserable as ever we please. And many do please to make themselves extremely miserable, i.e., to do what they know beforehand will render them so. They follow those ways, the fruit of which they know, by instruction, example, experience, will be disgrace, and poverty, and sickness, and untimely death. This every one observes to be the general course of things; though it is to be allowed, we cannot find by experience, that all our sufferings are owing to our own follies. [41]

Butler realizes that man does not have complete control of himself or his environment. But man, by the exercise of prudence can live comfortably under normal circumstances. Man's happiness is a result of his own actions as well as most of his misery. Man may not be able to have every enjoyment that he may want; but those he does experience come by his own efforts.

A new concept has been implicitly introduced by Butler in the second chapter, and it should be made explicit, even though its importance is not evident here. It is the concept of the "reasonable and prudent man." The reasonable man considers the future life only if it is connected with the present life; the reasonable man is able to foresee the consequences of his actions. The prudent man is the one who acts according to his reason so that he might obtain pleasurable consequences. Even though this concept is not elaborated in the present context, it is interesting to note its appearance here, since is will reappear throughout Butler's writings.

Although it will be remembered that in the last section Butler has little patience with those who speculate how the universe

[40] I, *Analogy*, chap. II, p. 48, para. 2.
[41] *Ibid.*

should have been made in distinction from the actual course of nature, he takes time out to give possible reasons why the universe is as it is in regard to his position that an individual's pleasures and pains are dependent upon his own actions. Why the author of nature does not make his creatures "happy without the instrumentality of their own actions, and prevent their bringing any sufferings upon themselves" [42] is a question, in itself impossible to answer; but suggestions, such as the following, are offered: (1) any other method may produce less happiness on the whole than the present method; (2) divine goodness may apply only to make the good, faithful, and honest man happy and not to produce happiness in general; (3) God may be pleased when his creatures act in accordance with their nature and the relations in which they are placed; or (4) the end for which God has created may be beyond the reach of human faculties.

"But however this be, it is a certain matter of universal experience, that the general method of divine administration is, forwarning us, or giving us capacities to forsee, with more or less clearness, that if we act so and so, we shall have such enjoyments, if so and so, such sufferings; and giving us those enjoyments, and making us feel those sufferings, in consequence of our actions." [43]

This is all to be ascribed to the general course of nature, or more correctly to the author of the course of nature. One characteristic of God's natural governorship of the universe is the uniformity or constancy of the course of nature. When this characteristic is viewed from the human perspective, the tendency is to think of this uniformity of the course of nature as natural, in opposition to supernatural, because of its constancy. Butler, of course, thinks that this should not be the case.

"Every man, in everything he does, naturally acts upon the forethought and apprehension of avoiding evil or obtaining good: and if the natural course of things be the appointment of God, and our natural faculties of knowledge and experience are given us by him; then the good and bad consequences which follow our actions, are his appointment, and our foresight of those consequences, is a warning given by him, how we are to act." [44]

[42] *Ibid.*, p. 49, para. 3.
[43] *Ibid.*, p. 50, para. 3.
[44] *Ibid.*, pp. 51-2, para. 4.

Perhaps this sentence is one of the best summaries of Butler's theistic position which has appeared so far in the *Analogy*. It has something to say about man, the universe in which man lives, and God. The phrase at the beginning of the sentence is descriptive in that it states that all men act to avoid evil and obtain the good; [45] but, since Butler links pain with evil and pleasure with the good in this context, we may restate the description in this manner: all men act to avoid pain and obtain pleasure. Why is this the case? This is the way that God has made man. But God has also made the universe in which man finds himself, and God has caused the universe and man to so function that man is able to obtain knowledge from his experiences. With the knowledge thus obtained, man is able to determine to some extent the consequences of his actions, and he naturally chooses that which obtains pleasure. By use of his reason, man is able to think ahead and pick actions that lead to pleasurable consequences and that are naturally desirable to him. Butler, however, goes beyond this description of events to add that God appoints the consequences of our actions as indications of how man is to act, and this addition is prescriptive and not descriptive. In this way, Butler is able to link duty and desire within his theistic framework, since man will act in order to obtain pleasure; but when he so acts, he is acting the way that he should act, since God has attached the pleasurable consequence to that action.

In this discussion, Butler is working toward the establishment of the proposition that God governs the actions of man in this present life by the uniform prearranged relationship of rewards and punishments that follow the various actions of human beings. However, Butler does not want to push this to the extent that it would mean that the pleasure which accompanies each particular gratification of a passion is an indication that the individual is being rewarded by means of that gratification. Rather, he wants to view this in the general sense in the same way that the function

---

[45] This seemed self-evidently true during the Enlightenment, but Professor Eliseo Vivas has expressed it that now we post-Freudians know how untrue it is.

of the eyes is to see, not that the eyes are supposed to look at each and every particular object that it is possible for them to see, since some things will destroy the power of sight. In the same manner that it is not doubted that in general the eyes are the organs of sight for the individual, so there is no doubt "that the foreseen pleasures and pains belonging to the passions, were intended, in general, to induce mankind to act in such and such manners".[46]

So far the argument that Butler is developing rests only on the supposition of the author of the universe as the natural governor, and as yet he does not join this concept of the natural governor with that of the moral governor of the universe. It is not necessary to do so because, according to Butler, the proper formal notion of government is to annex "pleasure to some actions, and pain to others, in our power to do or forbear, and giving notice of this appointment beforehand to those whom it concerns".[47] Since God does reward and punish as developed above, man is under his government in the same sense that he is under civil government. After an author of nature is presupposed, it is not only from deduction, but also from experience that man finds he is under the government of this same author. Seemingly in allusion to the exchange of ideas between Leibniz and Clarke, Butler goes on to note that it makes no difference to his development whether the pleasure and pain which follow as a consequence of our behaviour is due to God's acting on the individual when the pleasure or pain is experienced or whether this was established beforehand in the plan of the universe as a natural consequence. In either case, the individual is still under the government of the author of nature.

Throughout this development Butler's contention is that the pleasures and pains that are the consequences of actions are instances of final causes. The joint assumption of Butler and the deists involved a final cause, since they agreed that there was a creator of the universe. Now Butler wants to go on and say that the way that God has connected pleasure and pain with human

---

[46] I, *Analogy*, chap. II, p. 52, para. 5.
[47] *Ibid.*, p. 53, para. 6.

action is as good a way to indicate to man what he is to do as any other means.

> If, for example, the pain which we feel, upon doing what tends to the destruction of our bodies, suppose upon too near approaches to fire, or upon wounding ourselves, be appointed by the Author of nature to prevent our doing what thus tends to our destruction; this is altogether as much an instance of his punishing our actions, and consequently of our being under his government, as declaring by a voice from heaven, that if we acted so, he would inflict such pain upon us.[48]

Thus it is found that even before consideration of the moral nature of God is undertaken, he is recognized as the governor of the universe. If God rewards and punishes his creatures in this life by the means of pleasure and pain, there is nothing incredible in the general religious doctrine that God will act in a similar manner in the future life. All of this does not necessarily mean that in this life the pleasure and pain follow immediately upon the completion of the action, since experience teaches that this is not the case; in fact, there is often a long lapse of time. Because Butler thinks that the idea of punishment is the most cavilled, he choses his illustrative material from this area emphasizing the point that, although some seem to go along in life without receiving punishment for their misdeeds, punishment generally falls sooner or later since it is in the natural course of things and the frequency is enough to support the idea of punishment in the future life. Butler does not deal specifically with the instances that could be noted from experience of the wicked who prosper and who seemingly do not receive their just deserts during their life, but in some passages he mentions the fact of inward uneasiness. This would allow him to take care of this type of instance without appealing to punishment in a future life to straighten out the miscarriages of justice in the present life.

The affinity with tendencies in Locke's thought are easily seen.[49] In the next section, Butler will argue for the moral government of God and when this is established, he contends that

---

[48] *Ibid.*, p. 54, para. 8.
[49] Cf. p. 42 and p. 85 above.

this divine moral government assures that misery is the consequence of vice either in this world or in some future state by the righteous judgment of God. Just because we know this fact does not imply that we have any information concerning the reason why God has so decreed or how his decree will be executed. Since the method of execution is left open, there is no absurdity in supposing that it may be analogous to the matter in which certain consequences naturally follow in the present state of things, such as a fall may break a limb. Some may be offended by this analogy, but there is no basis for this, since even though things come to pass according to the course of nature, this does not exclude God, since he is also the God of nature.

D. THE MORAL GOVERNMENT OF GOD

Just as the evidence of design and of causes in the constitution of the universe proves it to be under the control of an intelligent mind, so the evidence of pleasure and pain distributed among creatures with sense and reason proves that these creatures are under the natural government of this intelligent mind. God's natural government of the world is the same as that exercised by a master over his servants or by a civil magistrate over his subjects. Butler uses this line of reasoning to establish that the intelligent maker of the universe is also the intelligent governor of it, and he thinks that this is conclusive. However, this conclusion does not say anything about the moral nature of God as a governor for a "moral government consists, not merely in rewarding and punishing men for their actions, which the most tyrannical person may do: but in rewarding the righteous, and punishing the wicked; in rendering to men according to their actions considered as good or evil".[50] The criterion, therefore, for a moral government is one in which rewards and punishments are distributed in exact proportion to personal merit or demerit. Now that Butler has established God as the natural governor of the universe, he turns in his argument to show that God is also the moral governor.

[50] I, *Analogy*, chap. III, p. 64, para. 2.

Contrary to some of the beliefs current in his time, Butler does not hold that the author of nature has only the single characteristic of absolute benevolence, and thinks that "we should speak with cautious reverence upon such a subject".[51] Butler does hold that God has constituted this world for the happiness of intelligent creatures, but this does not limit God's characteristics to benevolence. His purpose is not to prove or disprove this idea of benevolence, but to investigate whether or not it can be proved from the constitution and conduct of the world that there is a righteous government of the universe, for, any government implies a governor. This does not mean that Butler was looking for a perfect moral government in the present state of the world; rather, he was trying to find the extent "the principles and beginnings of a moral government over the world may be discerned, notwithstanding and amidst all the confusion and disorder of it".[52] In order to show that there is a righteous administration in the present life does not mean that virtue will always be happier than vice, but Butler maintains that this is usually the case. The inclusion of the idea of a moral governor along with that of the natural governor of the universe seems to harmonize most closely with man's natural sense of things.

Since it appears to be fact, that God does govern mankind by the method of rewards and punishments according to some settled rules of distribution; it is surely a question to be asked, What presumption is there against his finally rewarding and punishing them according to this particular rule, namely, as they act reasonably or unreasonably, virtuously or viciously?[53]

Butler naturally sees no presumption against this, and this seems to be the case because God has so made human minds. In this life, the general order of things is that tranquillity, satisfaction, and external advantage are the natural consequences of prudent management of ourselves and our affairs, and that rashness, negligence, and folly bring after them inconvenience and suffering and these facts point to the conclusion that there is a right constitution of nature.

[51] I, *Analogy*, chap. II, p. 65, para. 3.
[52] I, *Analogy*, chap. III, p. 66, para. 4.
[53] *Ibid.*, p. 68, para. 8.

And thus, that God governs the world by general fixed laws, that he has endued us with capacities or reflecting upon this constitution of things, and foreseeing that good and bad consequences of our behavior; plainly implies some sort of moral government; since from such a constitution of things it cannot but follow, that prudence and imprudence, which are of the nature of virtue and vice, must be, as they are, respectively rewarded and punished.[54]

In the natural course of things, the providence of God is carried out through human government by the instrumentality of men; it punishes vicious actions as mischievous to society and rewards virtuous actions as beneficial to society. Thus man finds himself unavoidably accountable for his behaviour. In some cases it may be pointed out that actions beneficial to society are punished by society and that mischievous actions are rewarded. When this happens, there is some misunderstanding, since a beneficial action is not punished when considered as beneficial, but when considered as harmful. "The Author of Nature has as truly directed, that vicious actions, considered as mischievous to society, should be punished, and put mankind under a necessity of this punishing them; as he has directed and necessitated us to preserve our lives by food".[55] If virtue as such is rewarded and vice as such is punished, then this is an instance of moral government. In order to clarify this, Butler distinguishes between the action itself and the quality of virtuous or vicious which is ascribed to that action.

The gratification itself of every natural passion must be attended with delight: and acquisitions or fortune, however made, are acquisitions of the means or materials of enjoyment. An action then, by which any natural passion is gratified or fortune acquired, procures delight or advantage; abstracted from all consideration of the morality of such action. Consequently, the pleasure or advantage in this case, is gained by the action itself, not by the morality, the virtuousness or viciousness of it; though it be, perhaps, virtuous or vicious. Thus, to say such an action or course of behaviour, procurred such pleasure or advantage, or brought on such inconvenience and pain, is quite a different thing from saying, that such good or bad effect was owing to the virtue or vice of such action or behaviour. In one case, an action abstracted from all moral consideration, produced its effect: in the other case, for it will appear that there are such cases, the morality of

[54] *Ibid.*, p. 70, para. 11.
[55] *Ibid.*, p. 71, para. 12.

the action, the action under a moral consideration, i.e., the virtuousness or viciousness of it, produced the effect. Now I say virtue as
such, naturally procures considerable advantages to the virtuous, and
vice as such, naturally occasions great inconvenience and even misery
to the vicious, in very many instances. The immediate effects of virtue
and vice upon the mind and temper, are to be mentioned as instances
of it. Vice as such is naturally attended with some sort of uneasiness,
and, not uncommonly, with great disturbance and apprehension. That
inward feeling, which, respecting lesser matters, and in familiar
speech, we call being vexed with oneself, and in matters of importance
and in more serious language, remorse; is an uneasiness naturally
arising from an action of man's own, reflected upon by himself as
wrong, unreasonable, faulty, i.e., vicious in greater or less degrees.[56]

This distinction allows Butler to handle situations that he would
want to classify as vicious although the situation affords pleasure
to the individual actor, even though Butler does not make this
usefulness explicit. God has assigned pleasurable consequences
to a certain act since this act is generally what man should do;
however, under certain conditions, man should not perform this
act. If the individual goes ahead and performs this act when he
should not, the pleasurable consequences will naturally follow
even though the act would be vicious under these specific circumstances. The pleasure comes from the act itself, not from the
virtue of the act. However, pleasure and pain are only a part of
the many factors of the moral government of the world which
guide men in their actions.

Besides the good and bad effects of virtue and vice upon men's own
minds, the course of the world does, in some measure, turn upon the
approbation and disapprobation of them as such, in others. The sense
of well and ill-doing, the presages of conscience, the love of good
characters and dislike of bad ones, honour, shame, resentment,
gratitude; all these, considered in themselves, and in their effects,
do afford manifest real instances of virtue as such naturally favoured,
and of vice as such discountenanced, more or less, in the daily course
of human life, in every age, in every relation, in every general
circumstance of it.[57]

In other words, each man faces the weight of the society in which

[56] *Ibid.*, pp. 72-3, para. 13.
[57] *Ibid.*, p. 76, para. 17.

he finds himself pushing him towards the actions that this society has classified as virtuous. When deciding whether or not to perform an action, this pressure, along with the pleasure and pain that will accompany the action, must be taken into account.

In addition to the teleological and cosmological arguments for the existence of God mentioned at the beginning of this section, Butler also holds that the moral argument is valid. The fact that God has given man a moral nature is a proof that man is under the moral government of God and that God "will finally favour and support virtue effectually".[58] The fact that God has put his moral creature man into a situation in this world so that he must act and the fact that God influences mankind to act virtuously by rewards is another argument supporting the contention that in this life man is under the moral government of God. Man's moral nature is so constituted "that peace and delight, in some degree and upon some occasions, is the necessary and present effect of virtuous practice",[59] and the moral nature is such that it is in harmony with virtuous action in the sense that "there is nothing in the human mind contradictory, as the logicians speak, to virtue".[60] When elaborating on the compatibleness of virtue with the moral nature and its incompatibleness with vice, Butler notes that "virtue consists in a regard to what is right and reasonable, as being so; in a regard to veracity, justice, charity, in themselves; and there is surely no such thing, as a like natural regard to falsehood, injustice, cruelty".[61]

This is all good and well, but what would happen in the case of someone who claims to have a natural regard for the vices which Butler lists above? First of all, he thinks that there are no such cases, but for the sake of argument he supposes that such a case would be possible. "It is evidently monstrous: as much so, as the most acknowledged perversion of any passion whatever."[62] The obvious conclusion that Butler wishes to draw is that from the individual's very nature and from his condition in the present

[58] *Ibid.*
[59] *Ibid.*, p. 77, para. 18.
[60] *Ibid.*, p. 77, para. 19.
[61] *Ibid.*, pp. 77-8, para. 19.
[62] *Ibid.*

world, "vice cannot at all be, and virtue cannot but be, favoured as such by others, upon some occasions; and happy in itself, in some degree".[63] Even if the condition of society should be such that virtue is not rewarded, this "cannot drown the voice of nature in the conduct of Providence, plainly declaring itself for virtue, by way of distinction from vice, and preference to it".[64]

In one of the above passages, Butler notes that there is nothing in the mind contradictory to virtue. It will be remembered that this technique of linking ethics and logic was prominent in Wollaston. This idea is picked up again by Butler in the following passage.

For our being so constituted as that virtue and vice are thus naturally favoured and discountenanced, rewarded and punished respectively as such, is an intuitive proof of the intent of nature, that it should be so: otherwise the constitution of our mind, from which it thus immediately and directly proceeds, would be absurd. But it cannot be said, because virtuous actions are sometimes punished, and vicious actions rewarded, that nature intended it. For, though this great disorder is brought about, as all actions are done, by means of some natural passion; yet *this may be,* as it undoubtedly is, brought about by the perversion of such passion, implanted in us for other and good purposes, even of every passion, may be clearly seen.[65]

There are a couple of other noteworthy items in this quotation, but they will not be elaborated here since Butler does not do so. One is that the mind intuitively knows that human nature is constituted for virtue, and the other is that all actions, both natural and unnatural, are done in accordance with the passions. Now, because the mind knows that human nature is constituted for virtue, so far as the individual human is virtuous, he is on God's side, the winning side, and co-operates with Him. "To such a man, arises naturally a secret satisfaction and sense of security, and implicit hope of somewhat further." [66]

Before moving on to a discussion of the "Dissertation on Virtue", the argument presented by Butler for the moral government of God will be summarized in his own words.

[63] *Ibid.*
[64] *Ibid.*, p. 79, para. 20.
[65] *Ibid.*
[66] *Ibid.*, p. 80, para. 21.

There is a kind of moral government implied in God's natural government: virtue and vice are naturally rewarded and punished as beneficial and mischievous to society; and rewarded and punished directly as virtue and vice. The notion then of a moral scheme of government is not fictitious, but natural; for it is suggested to our thoughts by the constitution of this scheme is actually begun ... And these things are to be considered as a declaration of the Author of nature, for virtue, and against vice: they give a credibility to the supposition of their being rewarded and punished hereafter; and also ground to hope and to fear, that they may be rewarded and punished in higher degrees than they are here ... And from these things together, arises a real presumption, that the moral scheme of government established in nature, shall be carried on much further towards perfection hereafter; and I think, a presumption that it will be absolutely completed. But from these things, joined with the moral nature which God has given us, considered as given us by him, arises a practical proof that it will be completed: a proof from fact; and therefore a distinct one from that, which is deduced from the eternal and unalterable relations, the fitness and unfitness of actions.[67]

Butler seems to be making the same distinction here between the *a priori* method of deduction and the *a posterior* method of induction from the facts of experience that he makes at the beginning of the *Sermons*. From the context here, it is quite obvious that he holds both methods to be valid, but that he has chosen to use the latter method. Butler's feeling was that the spirit of the age required an inductive apologetic. It will be recalled from the discussion of the other ethical theorists of Butler's day that the *a priori* method was used by his very good friend Samuel Clarke.

E. THE NATURE OF VIRTUE

In the first part of this chapter Butler introduces the concepts of "virtue" and "vice", which are important for him in Dissertation II, "Of the Nature of Virtue", which will be discussed here, since in the first edition it was included as part of the present chapter. The meaning which Butler wished to assign to these words is very difficult to determine from this section because of the various uses of them. In the first appearance the meaning seemingly is

[67] *Ibid.*, pp. 92-4, para. 38.

good and bad in their moral sense. "Now one might mention here, what has been often urged with great force, that in general, less uneasiness and more satisfaction, are the natural consequences of a virtuous than of a vicious course of life, in the present state, as an instance of a moral government established in nature." [68] Later the idea of reasonable is linked with virtue and unreasonable with vice. "What presumption is there against his finally rewarding and punishing them according to this particular rule, namely, as they act reasonably or unreasonably, virtuously or viciously?" [69] Still later, virtue and vice are paired with prudence and imprudence. "From such a constitution of things it cannot but follow, that prudence and imprudence, which are of the nature of virtue and vice, must be, as they are, respectively rewarded and punished." [70]

As the argument "Of the Nature of Virtue" is developed, perhaps these concepts will become clearer. This short passage of Butler is very well known in the study of ethics, but seldom is the chapter "On the Moral Government of God" mentioned, even though this was the original context of the dissertation. Butler made it into an appendix in the second and all succeeding editions, even though he considered it closely connected with the third chapter, because it did not directly come under the title of the *Analogy* and thus interrupted his sustained argument.

The dissertation opens with the position that man is different from the other living creatures in that he has the added capacity of reflection, which enables man to make actions and characters an object of thought. This potentiality of reflection, along with the natural and unavoidable judgment of its objects as virtuous and of good desert or as vicious and of ill desert, constitutes the moral nature of man, which has been given man by God. Evidence supporting this moral approving and disapproving faculty is found in the individual's own experience and is also recognized in the experience of other human beings. This moral faculty really has two different functions: (1) upon taking a survey of

[68] *Ibid.*, p. 66, para. 5.
[69] *Ibid.*, p. 68, para. 8.
[70] *Ibid.*, p. 70, para. 10.

an action, either before or after the act has been committed, the moral faculty determines that act to be good or evil, and (2) the moral faculty determines itself to be the authoritative guide of action as over against any other faculty or guide of action. This two-fold function is the same as that of the speculative reason which "*directly* and naturally judges of speculative truth and falsehood; and at the same time is attended with a consciousness upon *reflection,* that the natural right to judge of them belongs to it".[71]

What evidence can Butler propose to support his contention that there is such a thing as this moral faculty? He suggests four different kinds. (1) The evidence provided by language in that in every language there are pairs of words such as "right" and "wrong", "odious" and "amiable", and "base" and "worthy" that are applied to actions and characters. (2) The evidence from the judgments commonly made by man, even to the extent of approving or disapproving imaginary characters (as in a novel), as well as the distinction between an action that just happens to produce good and one that intended it, the distinction between injury and mere harm, and the distinction between injury and just punishment. (3) The evidence from the behaviour of man that is naturally based on the above judgment of approval or disapproval. (4) The evidence offered from the many written systems of morals that would be meaningless unless there was a distinction between such words as "good" and "evil". Again Butler goes to experience in order to offer evidence in support of his assumption: That man has a moral faculty is confirmed by experience.

When Butler discusses a name for this moral faculty, he makes it quite clear that the name chosen is unimportant.

It is manifest [that a] great part of common language, and of common behaviour over the world, is formed upon supposition of such a moral faculty; whether called conscience, moral reason, moral sense, or divine reason; whether considered as a sentiment of the understanding, or as a perception of the heart; or, which seems the truth, as including both.[72]

[71] I,"Of the Nature of Virtue", p. 398, fn.
[72] *Ibid.*, p. 399, para. 2.

Although the name may vary, he thought it obvious that there was such a moral faculty with the two-fold function of approving or disapproving and recognizing itself as having the authority to perform this function.

Because of this list of possible names, it is impossible to tell which Butler preferred in the "Dissertation", but in the *Sermons* he settled on conscience, and this term will be used here. It is interesting to note that he did not want to make an either/or choice between "a sentiment of the understanding" or "a perception of the heart", i.e., between making it a function of the intellect or of the emotions, but thought that the truth lay in somehow including both. At least the conclusion may be drawn that the conscience is not a separate entity of some kind in the body, but a function of at least the knowing and feeling aspects of the human organism. Likewise, it is not at all doubtful which course of action this faculty, or "practical discerning power with us" generally approves. Although there has been considerable dispute on the particulars of virtue, Butler maintains that there is a universally acknowledged standard of virtue.

It is that, which all ages and all countries have made profession of in public: it is that, which every man you meet puts on the show of: it is that, which the primary and fundamental laws of civil constitutions over the face of the earth make it their business and endeavour to enfore the practice of upon mankind: namely, justice, veracity, and regard to common good.[73]

It is obvious from this discussion that Butler never felt the force of cultural relativism, but of course, he wrote before such studies were of general interest. His outlook on the world is that of Eighteenth century provincial England. However, it is not necessary for Butler's position that justice, veracity, and regard to the common good be the actual situation under a civil constitution, but only that the civil constitution intends these ends, since Butler was far from regarding the present world as perfect. As a patriotic Englishman, he felt that the government of England best fulfilled these conditions, and that all civil constitutions tried to fulfill them at least to some extent.

[73] *Ibid.*, pp. 399-400, para. 3.

Butler feels that he has shown conclusively that man does have a moral faculty by which he discerns between good and evil, and now he wishes to elaborate this concept. In the first place, the conscience [74] has only one object which is human action, but in his idea of action, Butler includes the principles from which men act as well as the action as such. When these principles by which men act become habitual in any person, they are then thought of in the sense of the person's character. Whenever an individual is actually approving or disapproving an action, this is a deontological judgment for Butler, since, although the intention of certain consequences are part of the action itself, the fulfillment of these intended consequences in no way influences the approval or disapproval of the action.

Acting, conduct, behaviour, abstracted from all regard to what is, in fact and event, the consequence of it, it itself the natural object of the moral discernment; as speculative truth and falsehood is of speculative reason. Intention of such and such consequences, indeed, is always included; for it is part of the action itself: but though the intended good or bad consequences do not follow, we have exactly the same sense of the action as if they did.[75]

In other words, an action is approved or disapproved apart from the consequences that follow from the action, since the action itself is the only object of the conscience.

In the second place, when the conscience approves or disapproves an action, which means that the action is discerned as morally good or morally evil, it implies, at the same time, that the action is of good or ill desert. "It may be difficult to explain this perception, so as to answer all the questions which may be asked concerning it: but every one speaks of such and such actions as deserving punishment; and it is not, I suppose, pretended that they have absolutely no meaning at all to the expression." [76] But Butler is sure of one thing; when it is declared that the doer of an action should be made to suffer, the basis of

[74] Although Butler did not use "conscience" in the *Dissertation*, it will be used here in this discussion, because it was used by him in the *Sermons* and is so closely linked with his thought.

[75] I, "Of the Nature of Virtue", pp. 400-1, para. 5.

[76] *Ibid.*, p. 401, para. 5.

this declaration is not that it is for the good of society. The point of Butler's contention is that morally good actions deserve good deserts and morally evil actions deserve bad deserts.

For if unhappily it were resolved, that a man, who, by some innocent action, was infected with the plague, should be left to perish, lest, by other people's coming near him, the infection should spread; no one would say he deserved this treatment. Innocence and ill desert are inconsistent ideas. Ill desert always supposes guilt: and if one be no part of the other, yet they are evidently and naturally connected in our mind.[77]

Furthermore, Butler thinks that men generally judge the deserts of an action according to the circumstances. A weak regard to virtue that would enable a man to act well under normal circumstances would not be able to withstand the onslaught of temptation.

For in human creatures consisting chiefly in the absence or want of the virtuous principle; though a man be overcome, suppose, by tortures, it does not from thence appear to what degree that virtuous principle was wanting. All that appears is, that he had it not in such a degree, as to prevail over the temptation: but possibly he had it in a degree, which would have rendered him proof against common temptations.[78]

In the third place, the perception of vice and ill desert varies in accordance with the nature and capacities of the agent. This is perhaps best illustrated by the fact that in certain situations an individual's neglect to perform some action would be judged by all to be vicious in the highest degree. Another illustration offered in support of this point is as follows.

For, everyone has a different sense of harm done by an idiot, madman, or child, and by one of mature and common understanding; though the action of both, including the intention, which is part of the action, be the same: as it may be, since idiots and madmen, as well as children, are capable not only of doing mischief, but also of intending it. Now this difference must arise from somewhat discerned in the nature of capacities of one, which renders the action vicious; and the want of which, in the other, renders the same action innocent or less vicious: and this plainly supposes a comparison

[77] *Ibid.*
[78] *Ibid.*, p. 403, para. 6.

whether reflected upon or not, between the action and capacities of the agent, previous to our determining an action to be vicious.[79]

In the fourth place, Butler wishes to consider the individual's moral relation to himself in comparison with his relation to other people. Does an individual have any more right to neglect himself than he does to neglect others who are in his care? No! The very meaning of prudence for Butler was "a due concern about our own interest or happiness, and a reasonable endeavour to secure and promote it",[80] and such action is virtuous, since man approves such conduct in himself and others when judged in the calmest manner of reflection. Gladstone elaborates Butler's argument in this manner. If a man performs an action for the benefit of another individual, say x, this is benevolence and benevolence is a virtue. But if x now becomes the man's own self, the beneficial act is still the same done to one person instead of another. The act does not change its essential nature because it is now done for the benefit of the self rather than of another individual.[81] The facts of the case are, however, that man generally has such a sense of his own interest that he does not neglect his own good as much as that of others. But this does not change the fact that prudence is virtuous.

Not only does Butler wish to maintain that prudence is a species of virtue, but also that folly is a species of vice. "Folly" in this sense means "a thoughtless want of that regard and attention to our own happiness, which we had capacity for".[82] As evidence for this, the illustration is offered that man generally judges a person who is in a state of poverty after a long course of extravagance and unheeded warnings much more severely than a person who is in the same state through no fault of his own.

However, if any person be disposed to dispute the matter, I shall very willingly give him up the words virtue and vice, as not applicable to prudence and folly; but must beg leave to insist, that the faculty within us, which is the judge of actions, approves of prudent actions, and disapproves imprudent ones; I say prudent and imprudent *actions*

---

[79] *Ibid.*, p. 403-4, para. 7.
[80] *Ibid.*, p. 404, para. 8.
[81] *Ibid.*, p. 404, fn.
[82] *Ibid.*, p. 406, para. 10.

as such, and considered distinctly from the happiness or misery which they occasion.[83]

The fifth and last point that Butler makes in the Dissertation "Of the Nature of Virtue" is that "without inquiring how far, and in what sense, virtue is resolvable into benevolence, and vice into the want of it; it may be proper to observe, that benevolence, and the want of it, singly considered, are in no sort the whole of virtue and vice".[84] If it were the case that virtue was dependent entirely upon the amount or degree of benevolence and that vice was the absence of virtue, then the conscience would be indifferent to every other factor.

Suppose one man should, by fraud or violence, take from another the fruit of his labour, with intent to give it to a third, who he thought would have as much pleasure from it as would balance the pleasure which the first possessor would have had in the enjoyment, and his vexation in the loss of it; suppose also that no bad consequence would follow: yet such an action would surely be vicious.[85]

If virtue and vice are not dependent upon benevolence, how is the question, what are virtue and vice, to be answered? Is it correct to say that virtue and vice are determined by the approval or disapproval of the conscience? This seems to be what Butler is saying at the beginning of the dissertation when he asserts that the function of the conscience is not only to judge the act as virtuous or vicious but also to recognize itself as the authoritative guide of action. If it is proper to define "virtue" as that which is approved by the conscience and "vice" as that which is not approved by the conscience, then is it proper also to define the "conscience" as that which approves virtue and disapproves vice? If so, someone would be going in circles, and it is most certain that Butler did not want to do so. Butler holds that the conscience immediately approves or disapproves an action, but there are at least two possible interpretations to this position. One is that noted above which is that "virtue" means approved by the conscience and "vice" means disapproved by the conscience. The conscience legislates the classification of the

---

[83] *Ibid.*, pp. 406-7, para. 11.
[84] *Ibid.*, p. 407, para. 12.
[85] *Ibid.*, p. 408, para. 12.

action. The other interpretation is that the conscience approves an action because it is virtuous and disapproves an action because it is vicious. In this interpretation the conscience does not legislate virtue and vice but recognizes that an action is virtuous or vicious. Man as an entity is so constituted and the universe in which he finds himself is so constituted that the conscience as a function of man classifies actions as virtuous and vicious, and the conscience also recognizes that this is its proper function. When the theistic framework in which Butler was writing is recognized, there is little doubt that his interpretation was the second alternative.

The fact then appears to be, that we are constituted so as to condemn falsehood, unprovoked violence, injustice, and to approve of benevolence to some preferable to others, abstracted from all consideration, which conduct is likeliest to produce an overbalance of happiness or misery. And therefore, were the Author of nature to propose nothing to himself as an end but the production of happiness, were his moral character merely that of benevolence; yet ours is not so. Upon that supposition indeed the only reason of his giving us the above-mentioned approbation of benevolence to some persons rather than others, and disapprobation of falsehood, unprovoked violence, and injustice, must be, that he foresaw this constitution of our nature would produce more happiness, than forming us with a temper of mere general benevolence. But still, since this is our constitution: falsehood, violence, injustice, must be vice in us, and benevolence to some, preferable to others, virtue; abstracted from all consideration of the overbalance of evil or good, which they may appear likely to produce.[86]

So according to Butler, virtue is not equivalent to benevolence and vice the absence of benevolence at least from man's point of view. Even though man's moral nature is not merely that of benevolence, it may be that God has chosen as His end the production of happiness. Working on this supposition that God wishes to produce happiness in the world, he evidently foresaw that the best way to achieve the most happiness was through other means than to constitute human nature with the principle of general benevolence. Butler uses this idea that God has happiness of the universe as his end in this passage only as a sup-

[86] *Ibid.*, pp. 408-9, para. 13.

position, and it cannot be ascertained whether or not he thinks this is a plausible supposition. He uses it because such an opinion was held by some in his day. If it actually is the case that God has as his end the most happiness, this would be the best of all possible worlds, a concept used by Leibniz, a correspondent of Butler's friend, Samuel Clarke.

At the beginning of this chapter, Butler indicates that he will try to establish that in addition to being the natural governor of the universe, God is also the moral governor. His criterion of a moral government is one in which rewards and punishments are distributed in exact proportion to personal merit or demerit. The development of his discussion, especially in the dissertation has been to establish that man has a moral faculty by which he approves virtue and disapproves vice, and now Butler needs to bring these two concepts together.

Now if human creatures are endued with such a moral nature as we have been explaining, or with a moral faculty, the natural object of which is actions; moral government must consist in rendering them happy and unhappy, in rewarding and punishing them, as they follow, neglect, or depart from, the moral rule of action interwoven in their nature, or suggested and enforced by this moral faculty; in rewarding and punishing them upon account of their so doing.[87]

A moral government gives to each man his just deserts. Even though actual governments may fall short of this criterion, this is the function which they are trying to approximate. In the next section Butler will try to establish that God will take care of any inequities in the next life, since the purpose of the present state of existence is a preparation for the next state.

Before closing the dissertation, Butler asserts that the happiness of the world is the concern of God, which is an assertion that can only be made on the basis of a theistic framework, but he does not go to the extreme of the supposition above that this is the end which God has chosen for the world. The only way in which human being can promote the good of mankind is through the way God has established, i.e., through veracity and justice. In fact, it is the duty of each individual to try, within the limits

[87] *Ibid.*, p. 490, para. 14.

of veracity and justice, to aid the ease, convenience, cheerfulness, and diversion of his fellowmen. The problem is that man is so shortsighted in regard to future events that he can never be certain that the course of action that he has chosen will result in his anticipated consequences of an overbalance of happiness. It is man's duty, however, to act on this limited knowledge, since the most excellent of all of the virtuous principles is benevolence. This passage, which shows to such a great extent the kindly and practical nature of Butler, will be quoted in full.

The happiness of the world is the concern of him, who is the Lord and the Proprietor of it: nor do we know what we are about, when we endeavour to promote the good of mankind in any ways, but those which he has directed; that is indeed in all ways not contrary to veracity and justice. I speak thus upon supposition of persons really endeavouring, in some sort, to do good without regard to these. But truth seems to be, that such supposed endeavours proceed, almost always from ambition, the spirit of party, or some indirect principle, concealed perhaps in great measure from persons themselves. And though it is our business and our duty to endeavour, within the bounds of veracity and justice, to contribute to the ease, convenience, and even cheerfulness and diversion of our fellow-creatures yet, from our short views, it is greatly uncertain, whether this endeavour will, in particular instances, produce an overbalance of happiness upon the whole; since so many and distant things must come into the account. And that which makes it our duty is, that there is some appearance that it will, and no positive appearance to balance, this, on the contrary side; and also, that such benevolent endeavour is a cultivation of that most excellent of all virtuous principles, the active principle of benevolence.[88]

This seems as if it would be a good note on which to end the dissertation, but Butler adds an afterthought. It is a warning that, although veracity is one component of the rule of life, it is difficult to apply in everyday life. In addition to falsehood and deceit, in some cases a man may be obligated to do something which he foresees will probably deceive, even though he does not intend to deceive. But Butler goes beyond the problem to give the cause of the problem; he maintains that the cause is what today would be called the stratification of society.

[88] *Ibid.*, pp. 410-11, para. 16.

For it is impossible not to foresee, that the words and actions of men, in different ranks and employments, and of different educations, will perpetually be mistaken by each other; and it cannot but be so, whilst they will judge with the utmost carelessness, as they daily do, of what they are not, perhaps, enough informed to be competent judges of, even though they considered it with great attention.[89]

And, of course, this problem in semantics, which Butler pointed out, is still with us today.

The end of the Dissertation "Of the Nature of Virtue" has been reached as well as the end of the third chapter of the *Analogy* "Of the Moral Government of God". Before beginning the discussion on the present state of existence of human beings as that of probation, which implies trial, a brief summary of the argument so far will be given. Assuming that there is a God and that man is able to find out how he should act (both assumptions were current in Butler's day as shown by the discussion of the ethical thinking of his contemporaries), his first step is to establish that the present status of man's existence here upon the earth is only a part of his total existence. In other words, physical death does not end man's existence. The next step of the argument shifts to another subject and develops the idea that God governs man by means of rewards and punishments. Now it is the function of all governments to govern by rewards and punishments; so, this does not make the government of God a moral government. In order to be a moral government, the rewards and punishments must be administered justly, and in the third step Butler argues this point. In this part of his presentation, he also maintains the notion that man has a moral faculty by which he judges actions to be virtuous or vicious. Since God has constituted man with this moral faculty and the universe in which man finds himself, and since God is a moral governor, when man acts according to what he ascertains as virtue, he will be rewarded by God. The fourth chapter of the *Analogy* will develop the concept that the present state in which man finds himself is that of probation for the state which will follow his physical death as established in the first step of the argument. In other words, watch out! Your sins will be sure to find you out.

[89] *Ibid.*, p. 411, para. 17.

F. THE PRESENT STATE OF PROBATION

It is a general doctrine of theistic religion that the present life is a probationary period for the future life. For Butler, the most important idea in this concept is that man has at the present time possibilities for both good and evil behavior, and that therefore, his behavior is dependent to some degree upon the individual himself. Man experiences temptation to act viciously as well as having "inducements of reason" [90] to act virtuously. If man did not have this possibility of choice in his actions, there would be no ground for discriminating between his actions and judging them. Depending upon his good or evil behavior in this life, man will be judged by God, and rewarded or punished in the future life.

In the same manner, as under the moral government of God, man is in a state of trial with regard to his future life, so as under the natural government of God, man is in a state of trial with regard to his present life. His usage of "natural government" is that God annexes "pleasure to some actions, and pain to others, which are in our power to do or forbear, and in giving us notice of such appointment beforehand".[91] This ties in with Butler's development of the subject of the government of God by rewards and punishments in that man's present happiness or misery is dependent upon himself to some extent. When a man allows his passions to run away with himself so that he gratifies his passions at the expense of his wisdom and virtue, it turns out that his "particular passions are no more coincident with prudence, or that reasonable self-love, the end of which is our worldly interest, than they are with the principle of virtue and religion; but often draw contrary ways to one, as well as to the other".[92] In addition to the progression of the argument which is contained in this quotation, it is interesting to note that Butler seemingly uses "prudence" in this passage as equivalent with "reasonable self-love", which is that function of man which looks

[90] I, *Analogy*, chap. IV, p. 94, para. 1.
[91] *Ibid.*, p. 95, para. 2
[92] *Ibid.*, p. 97, para. 4.

out for his own interests in this life. Sometimes there are emotional overtones connected with the usage of "self-love" that may be avoided if thought of in the sense of "prudence". This concept is brought into the argument, since the prudent man will find it necessary at times to exercise self-control in the sense of denial in order to secure by the same means his present as well as his future good. Man may overcome his temptations, but he is constantly subject to them, which is what Butler means by probation. Not only is man continually liable to go wrong voluntarily, but from experience it is known that men actually do so with respect to both their temporal and religious interests. All of this points up the fact that temporal interests and religious interests are analogous to each other.

Although man has problems in both the temporal and religious realms, Butler singles out four difficulties and dangers in the religious state of trial: (1) the example of evil behaviour of other human beings, (2) an inadequate education at best and sometimes even morally wrong and vicious, (3) religions which have been corrupted into superstition, and (4) prior acts which put the individual at a disadvantage.

We certainly are in a condition, which *does not seem*, by any means, the most advantageous we could imagine or desire, either in our natural or moral capacity, for securing either our present or future interest. However, this condition, low and careful and uncertain as it is, does not afford any just ground of complaint. For, as men may manage their temporal affairs with prudence, and so pass their days here on earth in tolerable ease and satisfaction, by a moderate degree of care: so likewise with regard to religion, there is no more required than what they are well able to do, and what they must be greatly wanting to themselves, if they neglect. And for persons to have that put upon them, which they are well able to go through, and no more, we naturally consider as an equitable thing; supposing it done by proper authority. Nor have we any more reason to complain of it, with regard to the Author of nature, than of his not having given us other advantages, belonging to other orders of creatures.[93]

Because man finds himself in a state of probation in his natural capacity, it is reasonable to hold that an analogous state of probation exists in regard to his moral capacity.

[93] *Ibid.*, p. 102, para. 10.

[Since] thought and consideration, the voluntary denying ourselves many things which we desire, and a course of behaviour, far from being always agreeable to us; are absolutely necessary to our acting even a common decent, and common prudent part, so as to pass with any satisfaction through the present world, and be received upon any tolerable good terms in it: since this is the case, all presumption against self-denial and attention being necessary to secure our higher interest, is removed.[94]

In fact, the whole fourth chapter is devoted to the task of showing that "the thing here insisted upon is, that the state of trial which religion teaches us we are in, is rendered credible, by its being throughout uniform and of a piece with the general conduct of Providence towards us, in all other respects within the compass of our knowledge".[95]

As far as Butler is concerned, he has now established that man in the phase of his existence that he spends upon the earth is in a state of probation. In chapter six he develops the idea that this state of probation is intended for moral discipline and improvement. If someone should ask why it is that man is placed in a situation where so much difficulty is possible, it would be impossible to give a complete answer, and Butler wonders "whether it be not beyond our faculties, not only to find out, but even to understand, the whole account of this".[96] Butler does not want to face the problem of evil, so remarks only that some of the difficulties would be lessened if it would be observed "that all wickedness is voluntary, as is implied in its very notion; and that many of the miseries of life have apparent good effects".[97] Assuming for a moment that all wickedness is voluntary, this would not aid to any great extent the understanding of this problem, since this would deal only with moral evil and not touch natural evil, and certainly the difficulties which man faces are not all in the moral realm. The other remark that many of the miseries of life have apparent good effects fits in with the discussion[98] that it might be that God has as an end the greatest

---

[94] *Ibid.*, p. 103, para. 11.
[95] *Ibid.*
[96] I, *Analogy*, chap. V, p. 106, para. 1.
[97] *Ibid.*
[98] Above, p. 102.

amount of happiness. Because of our limited viewpoint, which is the same reason Butler gave for man not operating on the principle of benevolence only, man cannot see the whole context, and is thus open to misinterpretation. From God's point of view, the situation would appear differently.

But as our present condition can in no wise be shown inconsistent with the perfect moral government of God: so religion teaches us we were placed in it, that we might qualify ourselves, by the practice of virtue, for another state which is to follow it. And this, though but a partial answer, a very partial one indeed, to the inquiry now mentioned; yet, is a more satisfactory answer to another, which is of real, and of the utmost importance to us to have answered: the inquiry, What is our business here? The known end then, why we are placed in a state of so much affliction, hazard, and difficulty, is our improvement in virtue and piety, as the requisite qualification for a future state of security and happiness.[99]

Just as childhood is generally considered as an educational period for adulthood, so man's life in the present state of existence is an educational period for future life. In order to clarify this analogy, Butler proceeds to discuss a few observations that he wishes to make on this subject. In the first place, all different kinds of creatures are designed for a particular manner of life in that the nature of the creature corresponds to the external circumstances. If, for example, a man's capacities or his character were changed to a sufficient degree, he would be incapable of a human course of life. Human life and happiness in the present existence are a joint result of human nature and the environment of human life. "Without determining what will be the employment and happiness, the particular life of good men hereafter; there must be some determinate capacities, some necessary character and qualifications, without which persons cannot but be utterly incapable of it: in like manner, as there must be some, without which men would be incapable of their present state of life."[100]

In the second place, Butler points out that habits are formed by exercise. By practice, man may change his character, within

[99] I, *Analogy*, chap. V, p. 106, para. 2.
[100] *Ibid.*, p. 108, para. 4.

certain limits as is noted in the first observation, and acquires characteristics that he did not previously have. The third observation follows from the second as it points out that nature does not produce a mature human being, but that maturity is reached gradually and after a continued exercise of human capacities. In making this point, it is interesting to note the continued emphasis of practice and habit on the actions of a human being. Now these three observations can be made without any consideration of the moral government of God over the universe. When this is taken into consideration, the conclusion that Butler wishes to draw is easy to see; just as childhood is a preparation for maturity, so this present state of existence is a preparation for the future state. Since the government established in the universe is moral, so "virtue and piety must, in some way or other, be the condition of our happiness, or the qualification for it".[101]

Now Butler thinks that it is an obvious fact from experience that a human being is capable of moral improvement by discipline as well as it is obvious that even the best human beings are in need of improvement. "Mankind, and perhaps all finite creatures, from the very constitution of their nature, before habits of virtue, are deficient, and in danger of deviating from what is right; and therefore stand in need of virtuous habits, for a security against this danger." [102] The reason man is in danger from deviating from what is right is the nature of his own constitution.

For, together with the general principle of moral understanding, we have in our inward frame various affections towards particular external objects. These affections are naturally, and of right, subject to the government of the moral principle, as to the occasions upon which they may be gratified; as to the times, degrees, and manner, in which the objects of them may be pursued: but then the principle of virtue can neither excite them, nor prevent their being excited. On the contrary, they are naturally felt, when the objects of them are present to the mind, not only before all consideration, whether they can be obtained by lawful means, but after it is found they cannot. For the natural objects of affection continue so; the necessaries, conveniences, and pleasures of life, remain naturally desirable; though they cannot be obtained innocently: nay, though they cannot possibly be obtained

101 *Ibid.*, p. 119, para. 20
102 *Ibid.*, p. 121, para. 22.

at all. And when the objects of any affection whatever cannot be obtained without unlawful means; but may be obtained by them: such affection, though its being excited, and its continuing some time in the mind, be as innocent as is natural and necessary; yet cannot but be conceived to have a tendency to include persons to venture upon such unlawful means: and therefore must be conceived as putting them in some danger of it.[103]

But just as the tendency to deviate from the right is internal, so the safeguard from such deviation is also internal – the practical principle of virtue. This principle is capable of improvement by proper discipline and exercise; so that instead of following mere inclination, attention will be given to the situation in order to determine the right, and then this right course will be followed. "Thus the principle of virtue, improved into an habit, of which improvement we are thus capable, will plainly be, in proportion to the strength of it, a security against the danger which finite creatures are in, from the very nature of propension, or particular affections." [104] Since the government of the universe is moral in nature, any improvement in virtue must be an advancement in happiness, and the acquired habits of virtue and self-government are most likely necessary for the regulation of human affections even in the future state.

Since the passions which may tend to lead man away from the right are a part of his human nature, it is possible that human beings even if they would come from the hands of God without blemish, would be in danger of going wrong. The cultivation of virtuous habits would lessen this tendency, but would never eliminate it because it is part of man's nature. At this point Butler goes beyond a development of theism as such, and brings in a concept which is usually associated with Christian theism – depravity. Turning from the hypothetical case of a human being who comes unblemished from the hand of God but who yet needs to cultivate virtuous habits, Butler asks "but how much more strongly must this hold with respect to those, who have corrupted their natures, are fallen from their original rectitude, and whose passions are become excessive by repeated violations

---

[103] *Ibid.*, pp. 120-1, para. 23.
[104] *Ibid.*, p. 122, para. 24.

of their inward constitution"? [105] The latter need plenty of discipline, and the present state in which man finds himself provides the circumstances for such self-improvement in virtue and piety.

In an effort to defend this development against those (at least Shaftesbury) who would depreciate all religion related to hope and fear, Butler makes an interesting point that gives an insight into his whole system. The motive for improvement in moral discipline is unimportant. It may spring from self-love in the sense that it is in our own chief interest to be virtuous, or it may spring from hope and fear in the sense of doing what God commands just because he commands it, or again, it may spring from a constant regard to veracity, justice, and charity. "For, veracity, justice and charity, regard to God's authority, and to our own chief interest, are not only all three coincident; but each of them is, in itself, a just and natural motive or principle of action." [106] An individual may begin the good life and persevere in it from any one of these three motives, and as a result, his character will become closer to the moral constitution of nature and to the relationship that God maintains to it as the moral governor, and thus secure the happiness connected with such character. It often happens in Butler's thought that it is possible to start at different places but come to the same conclusion. The universe is an organic system with all of the various aspects interrelated.

In order to get around the problem that self-love may not always be coincident with the will of God as he affirms above, Butler adds the modification that self-love, in the sense of pursuing the individual's own interest, must be rightly understood. Due to the fact that God is sovereign over all, the individual, as a dependent creature, must submit to God. The habit of submission must be cultivated in order to keep self-love as well as the particular passions in line with divine appointments.

Butler ends his discussion of probation here and begins a new chapter in the *Analogy* "of the Opinion of Necessity, considered as Influencing Practice". This discussion does not seem to be

---

[105] *Ibid.*, p. 126, para. 30.
[106] *Ibid.*, p. 132, para. 36.

within the framework of his argument, but rather an apologetic against this possible objection to his development, and as such would be more in the nature of an appendix than in the body of the book. Gladstone notes that Butler probably included this section because "the idea was too prominent among the philosophical notions of the day to be simply passed by with safety. For he tells us that the opinion of necessity was the fashionable plea for unbelief".[107] Butler, however, included it in the body of the book, and it seems that it can be added to the discussion of probation, since, if the idea of necessity holds, then there is no such thing as probation in the present state as preparation for the future state. The details of Butler's apologetic will not be followed, but a few concepts which explicate his theistic framework will be noted.

The presupposition of the *Analogy* that there is an intelligent author of the universe who is its natural governor as well as its moral governor is reaffirmed.

Indeed we ascribe to God a necessary existence, uncaused by any agent. For we find within ourselves the idea of infinity, i.e., immensity and eternity, impossible, even in imagination, to be removed from our being. We seem to discern intuitively, that there must, and cannot but by somewhat, external to ourselves, answering this idea, or the archetype of it. And from hence (for this abstract, as much as any other, implies a *concrete*) we conclude, that there is and cannot but be, an infinite, an immense eternal Being existing, prior to all design contributing to his existence, and exclusive of it. And from the scantiness of language, a manner of speaking has been introduced; that necessity is the foundation, the reason, the account of the existence of God.[108]

Butler goes on to state that necessity in this sense applies only to God, which is, of course, a form of the ontological argument.

Butler also develops the argument for the existence of God from general consent. If a person by some process of reasoning or observation (such as Butler is attempting) becomes convinced of the truth of religion, that there is a God, who created the world, who is the moral governor and judge of mankind, and

---

[107] I, *Analogy*, chap. VI, p. 138, fn.
[108] *Ibid.*, p. 141, para. 4.

who will deal with every one according to his works, it would be natural for him to be curious about the history of religion in regard to its antiquity and to the number of adherents. This individual would find that this general system had been professed in all ages and countries from the very beginning. Since this is the case, religion came into the world either by being reasoned out or by revelation, and the weight of evidence points to the latter. The ontological argument and the argument from general consent can be added to the cosmological, teleological, and moral arguments developed earlier.

It seems strange that the first warning as to the limitations of the moral faculty should be included in this section. Butler observes "that as the speculative reason may be neglected, prejudiced, and deceived, so also may our moral understanding be impaired and perverted, and the dictates of it not impartially attended to".[109] This warning does not mean to cast any reflection on the speculative or practical faculties of perception, since it is their very nature to inform the individual in the theory of things and to instruct in how he is to behave as well as indicating the consequences of his behaviour. The warning is only to admonish the individual that he is liable in some degree to prejudice and perversion, and to be on his guard especially in regard to virtuous and religious actions.

In spite of the fact that there are difficulties in the concept of freedom of action necessary to Butler's argument, from experience, the individual feels that he does have freedom of choice and action within certain limits. Even though Butler denies the idea of necessity and its denial of religion, he attempts to restate the whole argument of the *Analogy* in such a manner as not to be affected by the opinion of necessity. A sketch of this endeavour will provide a good summary to Butler's whole argument.

It is a matter of fact that God governs the universe by a method of rewards and punishments and that God has given man a moral faculty by which he is able to distinguish between actions, approving some as virtuous and of good desert, and disapproving others as vicious and of ill desert. This ability of moral discern-

[109] *Ibid.*, pp. 155-6, para. 19.

ment implies a rule of action which carries its own authority in the sense that the individual cannot depart from its directions without being self-condemned. The dictates of this moral faculty, which are by its very nature a rule for the individual to follow, are moreover the laws of God, and the consciousness of this internal guide given to man by his maker, not only immediately raises a sense of duty to follow it, but also a sense of security when it is followed, and of danger when deviating from it. This consciousnes is the same thing as a command from God which implicitly includes the notion of rewards for obedience and punishments for disobedience, but when this is connected with the discernment of the moral faculty that deserts are connected with actions, the sanction is made explicit. It is most natural to think that on the whole, the government of God will correspond to this nature which he has given man, so that happiness will follow virtue and misery will follow vice.

That God will finally reward the righteous and punish the wicked is not concluded from man's reasoning that it is fit for God to act in this manner, but from the fact that God has told man that he will so act. He has done so through the fact that the notion of command carries with it the idea of reward and punishment as well as through the idea of good and ill desert discerned by the moral faculty.

However, I am far from intending to deny, that the will of God is determined, by what is fit, by the right and reason of the case; though one chooses to decline matters of such abstract speculation, and to speak with caution when one does speak of them. But if it be intelligible to say, that it is fit and reasonable for every one to consult his own happiness, then fitness of action, or the right and reason of the case, is an intelligible manner of speaking. And it seems as inconceivable, to suppose God to approve one course of action, or one end preferable to another, which yet his acting at all from design implies that he does, without supposing somewhat prior in that end, to be the ground of the preference; as to suppose him to discern an abstract proposition to be true, without supposing somewhat prior in it, to be the ground of the discernment. It doth not therefore appear, that moral right is any more relative to perception, than abstract truth is: or that it is any more improper, to speak of the fitness and rightness of actions and ends, as founded in the nature of things, than to speak of abstract truth, as thus founded.[110]

Although it may well be that God's actions are determined by the fitness of things, Butler is not interested in using this abstract approach as did his good friend Samuel Clarke.

G. SUMMARY AND CONCLUSION OF THE "ANALOGY OF NATURAL RELIGION"

Although the analogy of nature can establish the credibility of the general doctrine of religion, it has no way of establishing the wisdom, equity, and goodness of the divine government implied in the notion of religion. However, if it is supposed that God does exercise a moral government over the universe, the analogy of his natural government suggests that the moral government is a scheme that is beyond human comprehension. In fact, the natural government of the world is so complex a scheme that it is incomprehensible, but the connections observed lead one to believe that the natural government may be so connected with the moral government that together they make up one scheme. Butler's position is that the universe is just such a scheme, and thus it is possible to begin at any point within this scheme and work towards the author of this scheme who is God. Now if God's moral government is a scheme, each individual event must be adjusted beforehand with a view to the whole, and the human individual, basing his observations on the small parts of this whole that are within his range of vision, is an incompetent judge. For Butler, this human ignorance is "a satisfactory answer to all objections against the justice and goodness of Providence".[111] Just as our ignorance of relations in the natural government of God may lead an individual to speculate that an event cannot produce an effect that in experience it actually does, so our ignorance of the moral government of God may hinder our seeing that the most good is produced by events as they actually

[110] *Ibid.*, pp. 151-2, fn.
[111] I, *Analogy*, chap. VII, p. 167, para. 13.

are in experience than would be produced by the way an individual might think the moral government of the universe should be administered.

Even if our knowledge is limited, it is sufficient, as has been shown by the whole argument of the *Analogy,* to know that the individual does not cease to exist at death. This expectation of immortality opens possibilities beyond our present existence in regard to the happiness or misery each individual experiences to some degree in the present life. Since our present happiness or misery is dependent upon our actions, even though there may be a long lapse of time between the action and its result, it is reasonable to suspect that our future condition depends to some extent on our present actions. This natural government of God, under which each individual finds himself, necessarily implies some sort of a moral government in which each individual will be justly compensated for his actions. Although the complete account of why man is placed in his present condition is beyond our comprehension, religion at least gives part of an answer when it teaches that virtue and piety are ncessary qualifications for a future state of security and happiness under the moral government of God and that "the present state was intended to be a school of discipline, for improving in ourselves that character".[112] The reasonable man will recognize that this is the actual state of affairs and will act accordingly.

This concludes the development of the analogy of natural religion, which is only the first half of Butler's work. He has now completed his discussion of theism in general and turns to consider Christianity, which is a particular kind of theism.

H. THE ANALOGY OF RELIGION – THE IMPORTANCE OF CHRISTIANITY

If it is possible to reason as Butler has done so far concerning the state of moral affairs in the world, the question that follows concerns the need for the Christian special revelation which he

[112] I, *Analogy*, chap. VIII, p. 182, para. 8.

affirms. As Butler has done in some of the arguments discussed
in the first section of the *Analogy,* he assumes a position and
then goes on to give reasons for it. Here he assumes that a revelation has been given and then goes on to give reasons why such
a revelation is credible.

Indeed it is certain, no revelation would have been given, had the
light of nature been sufficient in such a sense, as to render one not
wanting and useless. But no man, in seriousness and simplicity of
mind, can possibly think it so, who considers the state of religion in
the heathen world before revelation, and its present state in those
places which have borrowed no light from it: particularly the doubt-
fulness of some of the greatest men, concerning things of utmost
importance, as well as the natural inattention and ignorance of mankind in general. It is impossible to say, who would have been able to
have reasoned out that whole system, which we call natural religion,
in its genuine simplicity, clear of superstition: but there is certainly
no ground to affirm that the generality could. If they could, there is
no sort of probability that they would. Admitting there were, they
would highly want a standing admonition to remind them of it, and
inculcate it upon them. And further still, were they as much disposed
to attend to religion, as the better sort of men are: yet even upon this
supposition, there would be various occasions for supernatural instruction and assistance, and the greatest advantages might be afforded
by them. So that to say revelation is a thing superfluous, what there
was no need of, and what can be of no service, is, I think, to talk
quite wildly and at random.[113]

A Christian revelation has been given; therefore, there must have
been a need for this revelation. This is of interest, since it is so
different from the previous development. Little hint has been
given before this point that man is not able to obtain all of the
information necessary for proper conduct by the proper use of
his reason. In fact, it seems that about the only way he can keep
from destroying his whole previous argument, after introducing
this limitation, is to hold that at the present time reason cannot
give information in all areas, even though at some past time, this
might have been possible. One such area is natural religion.

[Christianity] instructs mankind in the moral system of the world: that
it is the work of an infinitely perfect Being, and under his government;
that virtue is his law; and that he will finally judge mankind in

[113] I, *Analogy*, part II, chap. I, p. 198, para. 19.

righteousness, and render to all according to their works, in a future state. And, which is very material, it teaches natural religion in its genuine simplicity; free from those superstitions, with which is was totally corrupted, and under which is was in a manner lost.[114]

In fact, this republication of natural revelation for Butler in the Christian revelation is an authoritative publication, since it was supported by miracles, prophecy, and the establishment of the Christian church as a continuing witness to its importance.

But this is not the only function of Christian revelation. It also contains information that was always unavailable to man through the use of his reason. This revelation is of "a particular dispensation of Providence . . . [carried] . . . on by his Son and Spirit, for the recovery and salvation of mankind, who are represented, in scripture, to be in a state of ruin".[115] In addition to reaffirming natural religion, the Christian revelation gives positive commands that cannot be obtained by the use of reason.

By reason is revealed the relation, which God the Father stands in to us. Hence arises the obligation of duty which we are under to him. In scripture are revealed the relations, which the Son and Holy Spirit stand in to us. Hence arise the obligations of duty, which we are under to them.[116]

Just because in the nature of things man bears certain relationships to divine beings, he is under obligations of duty to them. Man knows his relationships to the first person of the Trinity through his reason, but he only knows of his relationship to the second and third persons through special revelation. But "how these relations are made known, whether by reason or revelation, makes no alteration in the case: because the duties arise out of the relations themselves, not out of the manner in which we are informed of them".[117]

However, the manner in which the individual becomes aware of a divine command is the key to the difference between positive precepts and moral precepts in religion. Moral precepts are differentiated from positive precepts in that the individual is able

[114] *Ibid.*, pp. 188-8, para. 5.
[115] *Ibid.*, p. 190, para. 7.
[116] *Ibid.*, p. 197, para. 17.
[117] *Ibid.*, p. 198, para. 19.

to reason to the nature of the case in a moral precept, while a
positive precept arises from external command and not from the
nature of the case. Positive precepts would not be duties at all
"were it not for such command, received from him whose creatures and subjects we are." [118] Even though the two kinds of
precepts can be distinguished, there is no difference in the obligation to follow them, since man is obligated to do both. Butler,
however, does discuss the possibility that a moral precept may
at times conflict with a positive precept, and when this is the
case, the moral precept has precedence over the positive since
the individual knows the reason for it. Moreover, a moral precept is also a positive precept because the Scripture supports
every moral virtue, and in this respect they are both upon the
same level. "But the moral law is, moreover, written upon our
hearts; interwoven into our very nature, and this is a plain intimation of the Author of it, which is to be preferred, when they
interfere." [119] This is clarified by the fact that Christ "from
whose command alone the obligation of positive institutions
arises, has taken occasion to make the comparison between them
and moral precepts; when the Pharisees censured him, for 'eating
with publicans and sinners'; and also when they censured his
disciples for 'plucking the ears of corn on the Sabbath-day'." [120]

According to Butler, the force of Christ's point against the
Pharisees was that they did not properly understand the Old
Testament Scriptures. If they had, they would have known that
the general spirit of religion consists of piety and virtue as distinguished from ritual observance. Moreover, man is under obligation to obey all of God's commands.

To these things I cannot forbear adding, that the account now given
of Christianity most strongly shows and enforces upon us the obligation of searching the scriptures, in order to see, what the scheme of
revelation really is; instead of determining beforehand, from reason,
what the scheme of it must be. Indeed if in revelation there be found
any passages, the seeming meaning of which is contrary to natural
religion; we may most certainly conclude, such seeming meaning not

[118] *Ibid.*, p. 203, para. 26.
[119] *Ibid.*, p. 205, para. 30.
[120] *Ibid.*, pp. 206-7, para. 32.

to be the real one. But it is not any degree of presumption against an interpretation of scripture, that such interpretation contains a doctrine, which the light of nature cannot discover; or a precept, which the law of nature does not oblige to.[121]

Again in this quotation, Butler repeats a thesis that reoccurs throughout his writings. Man is not to take an abstract approach to things, sit back and attempt to reason how he thinks the world is supposed to be or how he would have made the world if he were in control of creation. Rather, man is to start with experience and, by the use of his reason, build an explanatory framework for experience. This rational framework will never be complete because of man's finiteness, even though he is aided by a direct revelation from the creator.

Butler must now face the problem of incidents recorded in this revelation from God that do not harmonize with the principles of conduct that he obtains by his reason and that, for the most part, are reaffirmed by this same revelation. He attempts to handle this problem in the following passage.

Indeed there are some particular precepts in scripture, given to particular persons, requiring actions, which would be immoral and vicious, were it not for such precepts. But it is easy to see, that all these are of such a kind, as that the precept changes the whole nature of the case and of the action; and both constitutes and shows that not to be unjust or immoral, which, prior to the precept, must have appeared and really have been so: which may well be, since none of these precepts are contrary to immutable morality. If it were commanded, to cultivate the principles and act from the spirit of treachery, ingratitude, cruelty; the command would not alter the nature of the case or of the action, in any of these instances. But it is quite otherwise in precepts, which require only the doing an external action: for instance, taking away the property or life of any. For men have no right to either life or property, but what arises solely from the grant of God: when this grant is revoked, they cease to have any right at all in either: and when this revocation is made known, as surely it is possible it may be, it must cease to be unjust to deprive them of either. And though a course of external acts, which without command would be immoral, must make an immoral habit; yet a few detached commands have no such natural tendency.

I thought it proper to say thus much of the few scripture precepts,

[121] *Ibid.*, p. 209, para. 35.

which require, not vicious actions, but actions which would have been vicious had it not been for such precepts; because they are sometimes weakly urged as immoral, and great weight is laid upon objections drawn from them. But to me there seems no difficulty at all in these precepts, but what arises from their being offenses: i.e. from their being liable to be perverted, as indeed they are, by wicked designing men, to serve the most horrid purposes; and perhaps to mislead the weak and enthusiastic. And objections from this head are not objections against revelation; but against the whole notion of religion, as a trial; and against the general constitution of nature. Secondly, reason is able to judge, and must, of the evidence of revelation, and of the objections urged against that evidence.[122]

This passage seems to contradict Butler's previous discussion about conflicts between moral precepts and positive precepts; if a conflict should arise, the moral precept would have priority over the positive precept because the individual would be able to see the reason for the moral precept and not for the positive. But here he makes an exception; the same revelation, which above was said to affirm moral precepts by also making them positive precepts, is now said to give to particular individuals positive precepts that are contrary to moral precepts. These positive precepts require actions which generally would be classified as immoral and vicious, were it not for the positive precepts. However, Butler really does not want to say this; so he adds the modification that the positive precept, which is of course of divine origin, does not overrule the moral precept, but that the change concerns the relationship of the whole nature of the case and of the action, so that what previously would have been unjust and immoral, is not of this nature after the positive precept has been given. Although Butler does not explicitly say so, he must have some idea in mind that the individual to whom the positive command was given is acting as the agent of God, in some sense, akin to that of an executioner who acts as the agent of society while performing acts that otherwise would be regarded as crimes. If such is the case, then it seems that situations of this kind could only arise in a theocracy. The positive precept of God concerns only the external action, and does not promote

---

[122] I, *Analogy*, chap. III, pp. 239-40, para. 27-8.

the evil motivations usually connected with such an act when it is not commanded by positive precept.

This approach needs a framework, and on this occasion, Butler mentions what he has in mind. The only reason that man has any right to life or to property is because God has granted it to him; God as creator of the universe has created both people and things as well as the relationship of possession that may exist between them. When God has given the right of life to an individual as well as the right of possession of things, it is morally as well as positively (as is recorded in the revelation of God contained in the Christian Scriptures) wrong for any other individual to interfere with this relationship. However, if for some reason God should revoke this grant of life and of possessions, the individual has no other right to life or to possessions. In connection with this, if God should make this revocation known, as Butler holds that God has done in specific instances recorded in Scripture, it is no longer unjust to deprive such an individual of life or of possessions. In other words, murder is no longer murder, and theft is no longer theft. God has changed the situation.

Basically then, it is the will of God which makes a situation moral or immoral. Under normal circumstances, any individual, by the proper use of his reason, is able to ascertain what the will of God is, and the commands ascertained in this manner are called moral precepts. These moral precepts are reaffirmed in the Christian Scriptures, and the commands so ascertained become positive precepts as well as moral precepts. There are also some positive precepts contained in this revelation which cannot be known by the use of reason. Under normal circumstances, murder and theft are prohibited both by moral precepts and by positive precepts, but on special occasions, this is not the case. God, who has originally willed the grant of life and possessions, revokes this grant for some reason, and thus the individual affected no longer has any right to life or to possessions. When this decision of God is made known to another individual, the individual, to whom this revelation has been made, does not act immorally when he takes his possessions (under normal circumstances theft). God's will has changed the relationships of the situation.

How does the second individual know that he has received this personal divine revelation that God has revoked his original grant of life and of possessions from the first individual? Butler does not answer this question, but infers that this is the main objection which can be raised against this position. It is a fact of history that religious persecutors, thinking themselves to be acting for the cause of true religion, have performed acts normally classified as immoral. The actions when judged by moral precepts are evil; but it seems that there is no way for an observer to know whether or not these actions are done according to some positive precept given as a private revelation. According to Butler, there may be perversion when wicked, designing men, use the specific instances recorded in Revelation to serve their own horrid purposes. An observer has no way of evaluating, since the normal use of reason may have been overridden by God's positive command. Butler might want to segment history and to say that these cases of positive commands overruling moral commands should be limited to the instances recorded in Scripture. If he would, this would make some sense of the second assertion at the end of the quotation that reason is able and must judge the evidence of revelation and also judge the objections urged against this evidence. In this way, he is arguing for the whole and assuming that a certain few difficult parts are either unimportant or will fit into the whole. "When a supposed revelation is more consistent with itself, and has a more general and uniform tendency to promote virtue, then, all circumstances considered, could have been expected from enthusiasm and political views; this is a presumptive proof of its not proceeding from them, and so of its truth." [123]

But he does not think it incredible that assuming there is a revelation from God that it would contain things different from what would be expected. Nevertheless, everything contained in the revelation must be wise, just, and good, and, analogous to the argument noted in the summary of the *Analogy of Natural*

[123] *Ibid.*, p. 242, para. 30.

Religion,[124] "a sufficient answer to objections against the wisdom, justice, and goodness of the constitution of nature, is its being a constitution, a system, or scheme, imperfectly comprehended; a scheme in which means are made use of to accomplish ends; and which is carried on by general laws".[125] Any individual item of experience that might be pointed out as an instance contrary to wisdom, justice, and goodness from the human, limited point of view, might actualy within the total scheme of things, be instances of wisdom, justice, and goodness. It is obvious that there is no way of testing this assertion, if all negative evidence, which might be offered, is excluded. It again appears that such a line of argument would be acceptable only to those who already believe that wisdom, justice, and goodness are characteristics of God and of the universe created by Him, and that every seemingly contrary bit of evidence would not be so if seen within the total perspective, which is not available to the limited understanding of man. One of the basic assumptions of theism is that "the moral government of God is exercised by gradually conducting things so in the course of his providence, that every one, at length, and upon the whole, shall receive according to his deserts; and neither fraud nor violence, but truth and right, shall finally prevail".[126]

If the system of theism as an explanation is to be rationally coherent, it must handle to some extent events that the seemingly contrary to the scheme. Butler chooses to handle these by saying that if the individual were capable of viewing the whole, he would see how the individual pieces would fit into the scheme. It seems that he does not want to say that there is no such thing as evil, but that if there is evil, then it is the means to some good, or in other words, evil is a natural complement to the good.

This theistic scheme becomes Christian theism for Butler at this point, since the person and work of Christ is a "particular scheme under this general plan of Providence",[127] and the last part of the *Analogy* discusses particular problems, objections,

---

[124] Above, p. 117.
[125] I, *Analogy*, chap. IV, p. 243, para. 1.
[126] *Ibid.*, pp. 243-4, para. 2.
[127] *Ibid.*

and evidence in relationship to Christianity. After developing Christianity as part of the total plan of God, adequately fortified with quotations from the New Testament, Butler concludes as follows.

Now little, surely, need be said to show, that this system, or scheme of things, is but imperfectly comprehended by us. The scripture expressly asserts it to be so. And indeed one cannot read a passage relating to this 'great mystery of godliness', but what immediately runs up into something which shows us our ignorance in it; as every thing in nature shows our ignorance in the constitution of nature. And whoever will seriously consider that part of the Christian scheme, which is revealed in scripture, will find so much more unrevealed, as will convince him, that, to all the purposes of judging and object- ing, we know as little of it, as of the constitution of nature. Our ignorance, therefore, is as much an answer to our objections against the perfection of one, as against the perfection of the other.[128]

In a sense, Butler is here summing up again his whole purpose in writing the *Analogy*. He was writing against the deists who held that the individual's knowledge of God was limited to natural revelation, and that there was no such thing as a special revela- tion from God. But the same kind of objections that can be raised against the Christian Scriptures, can also be raised against the scheme of nature. Therefore, it is no more unreasonable to believe in one as in the other. This technique is used repeatedly in the second section of the *Analogy*. As an example, when arguing for the central message of Christianity that a mediator is needed, he contends that any argument against the idea of Christ as the mediator, is an argument against the general idea of mediation, which is useless, since the idea of mediation is generally accepted.

Butler states the objection to his analogical method of arguing as pointedly as could be done by any critic. To solve the difficul- ties in revealed religion by saying that the are the same difficulties met in natural religion is a poor way to handle the matter.

What is wanting is to clear both of them of these their common, as well as other their respective, difficulties; it is a strange way indeed of convincing men of the obligations of religion, to show them that

[128] *Ibid.*, pp. 245-5, para. 3.

they have as little reason for their worldly pursuits: and a strange way of vindicating the justice and goodness of the Author of nature, and of removing the objections against both, to which the system of religion lies open, to show, that the like objections lie against natural providence; a way of answering objections against religion, without so much as pretending to make out, that the system of it, or the particular things in it objected against, are reasonable – especially, must this be thought strange, when it is confessed that analogy is no answer to such objections: that when this sort of reasoning is carried to the utmost length it can be imagined capable of, it will yet leave the mind in a very unsatisfied state: and that it must be unaccountable ignorance of mankind, to imagine they will be prevailed with to forego their present interests and pleasures, from regard to religion, upon doubtful evidence.[129]

It is obvious that Butler would not bring up these objections himself unless he thought that he was able to handle them, and he answers in three ways. The first answer follows from the fact that he is arguing against the deists, and Butler claims that it is inconsistent to accept natural religion but reject revealed religion when they are both open to like objections. In addition, Christianity is vindicated chiefly from its analogy to the experienced constitution of nature and not only from its analogy to natural religion. The second answer is that religion is a practical thing, and it is his purpose to show that it is to man's advantage to take care of his religious affairs in much the same manner as it is to his advantage to take care of his temporal affairs. The third answer is that the purpose of the treatise is not to vindicate the character of God, but to show man his obligations and what he is to do. Religion presupposes at least a certain degree of integrity and honesty in those who embrace religion, in much the same way as it is presupposed that a man understands the language when someone speaks to him. The evidence for religion is sufficient for proper action; proof would require omniscience. Most decisions are made only on the basis that to follow a certain course of action will in all likelihood be in the actor's interest and happiness.

This concludes the discussion of the theistic framework of

[129] I, *Analogy*, chap. VIII, p. 354, para. 2.

Butler's thought taken from the *Analogy*. The *Sermons*, which are mainly on ethical subjects will be discussed in connection with this theistic framework. When his writings are so interpreted, they fall into the most systematic and consistent development of any of the initially alternative approaches.

VI

THEISM AND ETHICS IN THE *SERMONS*

A. INTRODUCTION

Although Butler is best known for his *Analogy,* it arouses little interest today, but his *Sermons,* especially the first three, are still read. Most books on apologetics have a rather limited temporal appeal, since they are written to combat some particular situation, as in the case of Butler, who wrote the *Analogy* against deism. The *Analogy,* however, proved to be an exception, since its appeal lasted until around 1860 when it was dropped as a classic at Oxford. During the Nineteenth century, it was one of the most widely reprinted books in the English language; the British Museum catalog lists, in addition to five editions of Butler's complete works, twenty eight editions of the *Analogy* and six of the *Sermans,*[1] and this does not include American publications.

Now the times have changed and there is little interest in reading a book written against deism when deism is no longer influential. Butler also was able to begin with some conception of the existence of God as has been shown by a review of the ethical thinkers of his time; but an effective apologetic in the present age would most likely begin at some other point, since God's existence is not a commonly accepted proposition today. If this is the case with the *Analogy,* why are the *Sermons* still popular to some extent? It seems that it is the method used in the ethical sermons, rather than the material content of his ethical theories that give them their lasting value. Butler attempts an empirical description of the psychology of ethical decision; he chooses to

[1] Ernest Mossner, *Bishop Butler and the Age of Reason* (New York: Macmillan Co., 1936), p. 197.

begin with man and his experience and build from this starting
point.The actual psychological description that he gives would,
no doubt, no longer be acceptable, but his empirical method is
certainly in the stream of British philosophy. But this method of
appeal to empirical experience is not something new in the *Sermons*; it was also used in the *Analogy*. In fact, the *Sermons* may
be only a more particular application of Butler's approach
throughout the *Analogy*. Because the *Analogy* is rarely read any
more and because theology is of less interest to philosophical
thinkers at the present time than it was earlier, this similarity
seems to have been overlooked. The following summary of Butler's approach supports this contention.

With limited intelligence in a universe of almost infinite facts, how
shall we *order* our lives? What shall be our *guide?* If we had the
mind of God, the problem would cease to exist, but His mind we do
not possess. Locke proved to us that we cannot appeal to any *inner
guide* such as innate ideas. Nor can we appeal *directly* to revelation
for we must have some prior basis of determining a genuine one from
a false one. Nor can we appeal to *mystical* experience for that is not
clear reason nor will Locke permit it. Our only recourse is to
experience – personal and the general store of humanity recorded in
such things as history books and books of natural science. Further,
by experience we mean primarily sense experience, although social
experience is not to be denied.

Some principle must be introduced to organize or to interpret
experience, *so that experience can guide our lives.* In our experience
we notice things are *similar* to each other. We observe certain
sequences in natural processes that are *similar* experiences with our
own body, and they follow the same sequential development. We
notice in personal biography that when people make certain deter-
minations certain consequences usually follow. We are aware of the
phenomena of nature with their similarities and likely consequences.

Our first task is to find experiences that are similar, or to use
Butler's word, *likely.* We presume then that this constitutes a more
or less reliable sequence . . . Each of us as we proceed through life
collects hundreds upon hundreds of similarities and forges them into
practical rules of conduct. These similarities forged into general
maxims of conduct constitute the *principles of guidance* through the
welter of experience.[2]

[2] Bernard Ramm, *Types of Apologetic Systems* (Wheaton: Van Kampen
Press, Inc., 1953), p. 123. Permission to quote granted by Bernard Ramm.

Because of his very nature, man is restricted to partial knowledge, and his principles of action must be formed from within this limited knowledge. The reasonable man is the one who guides himself by this limited knowledge, although the reliability of the principles of conduct may vary from a low to a high degree of probability. Man must guide himself in the every day activities of life by this limited knowledge, and he cannot expect any other source of guidance in ethical and religious spheres of life. The prudent man recognizes the analogy between the normal course of nature and the less known spheres of natural and revealed theology and realizes that he must act in the latter two spheres on the basis of inadequate knowledge in the same manner as he must do in the sphere of the normal course of things.

It should again be noted that Butler's use of analogy is only valid on the basis of his metaphysical presupposition that the universe is a unified whole. The natural governor of the universe is the same as the moral governor and similarities in administration are to be expected. This same natural and moral governor of the universe is also the author of the special revelation given to man, which is a republication of the content of natural revelation plus additional information that cannot be obtained from the natural revelation. Because the universe is a unified whole, a man is able to begin with most any aspect of it and reason to the principles guiding the whole as well as the author of these principles.

There seems to be the implicit assumption in the modern attention given to Butler that his ethical theories can be divorced from the other phases of his thought. It is obvious that a division can be made, but the separation raises the question whether or not this is a legitimate separation. On the basis of the method used in the analogy, which is only valid if the universe is an organic whole, the answer would be that the separation is not valid. The idea of an organic whole may imply that an investigation may begin at any place within the organism; but it also implies that knowledge of any one part of the organism is incomplete without knowledge of the relationships that the part under consideration maintains with the other parts of the organ-

ism. By the method of analogy, Butler tries to show what some
of these relationships might be. This problem is part of the larger
question that asks whether or not a consistent theist can ever
have an autonomous ethic or whether a theistic ethic is always
ultimately reducible to some aspect of God. By the very conception of theism, the latter alternative seems to be the only
ultimate opinion, and whatever else may be said of Butler, he
at least is attempting to argue for theism. The very form of his
ethical discourses betray this since they are a random collection
of sermons preached in the Rolls Chapel.

There is no better way to open a discussion of Butler's ethical
theory than to quote his paragraph in the "Preface" to the *Sermons* where he discusses the two different methods of approaching ethics.

There are two ways in which the subject of morals may be treated.
One begins from inquiring into the abstract relations of things: the
other from a matter of fact, namely, what the particular nature of
man is, its several parts, their economy or constitution; from whence
it proceeds to determine what course of life it is, which is correspondent to this whole nature. In the former method the conclusion
is expressed thus, that vice is contrary to the nature and reason of
things: in the latter, that it is a violation or breaking in upon our
own nature. Thus they both lead us to the same thing, our obligations
to the practice of virtue; and thus they exceedingly strengthen and
enforce each other. The first seems the most direct formal proof,
and in some respects the least liable to cavil and dispute: the latter is
in a peculiar manner adapted to satisfy a fair mind: and is more easily
applicable to the several particular relations and circumstances in life.[3]

It is generally thought that Butler had Clarke in mind as a representative of the first method and Shaftesbury as a representative
of the second. Another indication of his organic view of the
universe is his admission that whether the starting point is chosen
to be the abstract relation of things or the concrete facts of
experience, they both lead to the same conclusion that man is to
practice virtue. The characteristic attributed by Butler to the
second method is that it is adapted to satisfy a fair mind, and
since this has been his whole approach in the *Analogy,* Butler is

[3] II, *Sermons,* "Preface", pp. 5-6, para.

consistent in choosing this also as his approach in the *Sermons*.
Although Butler recognized that both approaches have advantages, he chose the second, and the suggestion is made here that this approach lends itself much more readily to homiletical technique than the other approach. The first three sermons proceed wholly on this approach. "They were intended to explain what is meant by the nature of man, when it is said that virtue consists in following, and vice in deviating from it; and by explaining to show that the assertion is true." [4] It seems that Butler is attempting to reach the man-on-the-street by an appeal to the facts of experience rather than to an abstract argument, even though his audience was perhaps as sophisticated as any church audience in his day.

Without naming any one in particular, Butler appeals to the ancient moralists who pictured man as possessing a definite nature. This human nature has virtue as the end to be pursued, and this is the same thing as following nature. Although Butler thought this was a rather common feeling among men of different ages, he thinks it necessary to give a detailed argument for it, which he does especially in Sc mons II & III. In the preface he sketches the outline he will use ɔ do this. Anyone who seriously considers the idea of the constit tion of a particular thing will come to see that it is a whole made up of several parts with certain various relationships holding between the parts. "Every work both of nature and of art is a system: and as every particular thing, both natural and artificial, is for some use of purpose out of and beyond itself, one may add, to what has been already brought into the idea of a system, its conduciveness to this one or more ends." [5] As evidence for this contention, Butler elaborates the well-known simile to a watch. Now this conception that the nature of things is related to some end is not restricted to the realm of things, but is also applicable to man.

Thus it is with regard to the inward frame of man. Appetites, passions, affections, and the principle of reflection, considered merely as the several parts of our inward nature, do not at all give us an idea of the

[4] *Ibid.*, p. 6, para. 8.
[5] *Ibid.*, p. 8, para. 10.

system or constitution of this nature; because the constitution is formed by somewhat not yet taken into consideration, namely, by the relations which these several parts have to each other; the chief of which is the authority of reflection or conscience. It is from considering the relations which the several appetites and passions in the inward frame have to each other, and, above all, the supremacy of reflection or conscience, that we get the idea of the system or constitution of human nature.

And from the idea itself it will as fully appear, that this our nature, i.e., constitution, is adapted to virtue, as from the idea of a watch it appears that its nature, i.e., constitution or system, is adapted to measure time.[6]

So far, Butler is giving a definition of the nature of a thing or being and is not describing any particular fact of experience, since any thing or being may be out of order. Now Butler is not so much interested in things as he is in human beings, and a crucial difference is that a thing is inanimate and passive, while a human being is an agent. Since a human being acts under his own power, he is accountable for any disorder, but when he is functioning properly as a human being, it is found that virtue is in accordance with the nature of man and vice contrary to it.

Although Butler is convinced that almost every man feels that virtue consists in following nature, when it is put into the form of an argument as he attempts to do in the first three sermons, the reasoning may be hard to follow. Because of this, he summarizes the whole argument in the preface. In common with brute creatures, man has various principles of action that lead directly either to the good of the community or to private good. But in addition, man has some principles of action that brute creatures do not have "particularly reflection or conscience, and approbation of some principles or actions, and disapprobation of others".[7] In the same manner as brute creatures obey their instincts or principles of action according to rules determined by the constitution of their body and the immediate environment, so most men obey their instincts and all of their principles. The important word here for Butler is "all".

---

[6] *Ibid.*, pp. 9-10, paras. 12-3.
[7] *Ibid.*, p. 12, para. 15.

It is not a true representation of mankind to affirm, that they are wholly governed by self-love, the love of power and sensual appetites: since, as on the one hand they are often actuated by these, without any regard to right or wrong; so on the other it is manifest fact, that the same persons, the generality, are frequently influenced by friendship, compassion, gratitude; and even a general abhorrence of what is base, and liking of what is fair and just, takes its turn amongst the other motives of action.[8]

But in order to have an adequate account of man's nature, it must be added that one of the principles of action, conscience or reflection, has a higher status than the others and exercises authority over the others so as to allow or to forbid their gratification. If the absolute authority of the conscience is not recognized, then man is not acting according to the constitution of his nature. To show that this recognition of conscience is necessary, Butler refers to Lord Shaftesbury's *Inquiry Concerning Virtue.* Butler agrees with Shaftesbury that virtue is naturally the interest or happiness of man and vice the misery, but what would happen in a situation where some man did not agree with this?

But suppose there are particular exceptions; a case which this author was unwilling to put, and yet surely it is to be put: or suppose a case which he has put and determined, that of a sceptic not convinced of this happy tendency of virtue, or being of a contrary opinion. His determination is, that it would be *without remedy*.[9]

To bring out a situation which your opponent's system seemingly does not cover and then to show that your system will take account of this situation is one of the most powerful means of philosophic argument. In the above situation Butler thinks that if the man were convinced that virtue did not lead to happiness, then he would be under an obligation to act viciously since one's own interest is an obligation. In order to insure that man will hold that happiness lies in virtuous action, Butler gives the conscience authority to rule in the matter.

For the natural authority of the principle of reflection is an obligation the most near and intimate, the most certain and known: whereas the contrary obligation can at the utmost appear no more than probable; since no man can be *certain* in any circumstance that vice

[8] *Ibid.,* para. 16.
[9] *Ibid.,* p. 15, para. 20.

is his interest in the present world, much less can he be certain against another: and thus the certain obligation would entirely supersede and destroy the uncertain one; which yet would have been of real force without the former.[10]

Shaftesbury was considerably more optimistic in his conception of man than Butler, so Butler needs an inner authority which will choose the virtuous life for man.

The Cambridge Platonists and the rationalists seemingly were not bothered with this problem, since good was some objective event that man could know, and once man had correct knowledge of the situation, he would act in conformity to it. As has been mentioned above, the moral sense philosophers share this optimism, but with the conception that good is felt rather than intellectually apprehended, and if man's feeling apparatus is functioning properly, he will follow its inclination. But Butler is a theologian as well as an ethical theorist, and although seemingly at times incompatible with his development, he retains the conception that all is not right with man. Man has inclinations which are not in harmony with his nature, and in order to keep them in control, there must be some authority to keep man acting in harmony with his constitution. The obvious question which follows would be to ask how the conscience of man is able to function properly if some of the other aspects of man are in disorder? Butler could make this an *ad hoc* assumption of his explanation, but later on it will be seen that this is integrated into his theistic framework by conceiving that the conscience is the voice of God within man.

As this study proceeds into the *Sermons,* it must be remembered that each of these writings is precisely that – a sermon. A. E. Taylor ably summarizes this point in the following quotation, and then he proceeds to point out the common assumptions of Butler and his congregation.

We must remember that these Sermons are what they profess to be, actual discourses addressed to audiences of educated citizens of London in the last years of George I., a body with perfectly definite education and social traditions. For the purpose in hand, it is irrelevant to dwell on minor differences between the moral convictions of in-

[10] *Ibid.,* p. 16, para. 21.

dividual members of the audience. It is quite certain that in all essentials Butler's hearers would be agreed (as educated citizens of the same age, the same class, the same language, and the same historical traditions must necessarily be agreed), on the question what sort of conduct is right and what is wrong. The question Butler rightly reckons with as the one which will be raised is not what it is that 'conscience' tells us to do, but why we should do it if we are minded otherwise.[11]

Taylor then turns to the two points of agreement between Butler and his audience.

We know what 'virtue' is, and we are agreed that the reasonable and right course of life is to live 'conformably to our nature'. The only point disputed . . . is whether the way of living which is admitted to be 'virtue' is or is not that which is conformable to our 'nature'. Butler does not consider the possibility of conflicting codes and the grounds on which a choice could be made between them; and rightly not, because he knows that his audience will not justify their misdeeds, after the fashion of Shelley's coterie in a later generation, by arguing that they are 'virtuous' when judged by the standard of the 'higher morality'. The early Georgian man of the world was too full-blooded a sinner to take that line of defense.[12]

B. SERMONS ON HUMAN NATURE

Butler begins his sermons with a text of Christian Scripture that is briefly expounded in order to show its connection to his development before moving into the discussion of conduct which in all case seems to be his primary concern. The text for Sermon I is Romans 12:4-5: "For as we have many members in one body, and all members have not the same office; so we, being many, are one body in Christ, and every one members of another." However, the meaning of this text is clearer in the Goodspeed translation than in the King James used by Butler. "For just as there are many parts united in our human bodies, and the parts do not all have the same function, so, many as we are, we form one body through union with Christ, and we are individually

[11] A. E. Taylor, *Philosophical Studies* (London: Macmillan & Co., Ltd., 1934), p. 296.
[12] *Ibid.*, p. 297.

parts of one another." [13] The intent of this passage is that in the same manner as each individual body has different parts which function as an organism, so the church, which is composed of individual beings, should function together as the mystical organism of the body of Christ. Butler, however, does not stick to this comparison between the individual body and the church, but enlarges the idea of the church to that of the whole society, and defends this enlargement of the comparison by noting that the conditions of the primitive Christian church were different from the Church of England of his day. If this is allowed, Butler's point immediately follows: each individual should do good to others in the society as the various individual parts of the human body function for the good of the whole body. But Butler is not through tampering with the text. Since there is little ground for comparison between a material body and society, and since the writer speaks of distinct offices, which according to Butler implies mind, it is allowable to substitute the whole nature of man with its variety of internal principles.

And then the comparison will be between the nature of man as respecting self, and tending to private good, his own preservation and happiness; and the nature of man as having respect to society, and tending to promote public good, the happiness of that society. These ends do indeed perfectly coincide; and to aim at public and private good are so far from being inconsistent, that they mutually promote each other . . .

From this review and comparison of the nature of man as respecting self, and as respecting society, it will plainly appear, that there are as real and the same kind of indications in human nature, that we were made for society and to do good to our fellow-creatures; as that we were intended to take care of our own life and health and private good: and that the same objections lie against one of these assertions, as against the other.[14]

The fascinating thing about this development is the trouble which Butler goes through to link his analysis of man's relationship to himself and to society with a passage of Scripture. The apparent reason is that Butler wishes to show that his analysis is com-

---

[13] *The New Testament*, trans. by Edgar J. Goodspeed (Chicago: University of Chicago Press, 1923), pp. 306-7.

[14] II, Sermon I, pp. 34-5, para. 3.

patible with the theism of the "inspired writers" [15] of Scripture. Butler now has two different principles in his first category: benevolence, "any affection in human nature, the object and end of which is the good of another", [16] and self-love, which has as its object and end the good of the self. Benevolence is a natural principle in man, although it will vary in intensity from individual to individual, in the same manner as self-love is a natural principle. Although the two are distinct principles as described here, they are so perfectly coincident that the greatest happiness of the individual will come from a balanced satisfaction of both.

In his analysis of human nature Butler differentiates another category of internal principles that he calls the several passions and affections. The reason for this double name is not stated, but he may intend a difference in degree of desire with passion the stronger. Although he makes a distinction between those that have as their intention the good of society and those that have the good of the individual, the same word "passion" is used of both, and a third seemingly synonymous name, "appetites", is also used in the discussion. Whatever name is used, this category of internal principles is "in the hands of Providence, to carry on ends, the preservation of the individual and good of society", [17] whether or not the individual is aware of these ends.

The sum is, men have various appetites, passions, and particular affections, quite distinct both from self-love and from benevolence: all of these have a tendency to promote both public and private good, and may be considered as respecting others and ourselves equally and in common: but some of them seem most immediately to respect others, or tend to public good; others of them most immediately to respect self, or tend to private good; as the former are not benevolence, so the latter are not self-love: neither sort are instances of our love either to ourselves or others; but only instances of our Maker's care and love both of the individual and the species, and proofs that he intended we should be instruments for good to each other, as well as that we should be so to ourselves. [18]

The third category in this analysis of human nature is the prin-

[15] *Ibid.*, p. 33, para. 2.
[16] *Ibid.*, p. 38, para. 4.
[17] *Ibid.*, p. 41, para. 6.
[18] *Ibid.*

ciple of reflection that distinguishes between human actions and approves or disapproves them, since man is so constituted that he reflects upon his own nature. Another name for this faculty is "conscience", and its function is to restrain men from doing evil and to lead men to do good to one another. The obvious conclusion that Butler wishes to draw from this analysis is that man is "made for society, and to promote the happiness of it; as that we were intended to take care of our own life, and health, and private good".[19]

This analysis of human nature shows that man is a social creature and that he attains his own best interests only in relationship to other human beings. In opposition to those who held that all of man's actions could be reduced to self-love, Butler contends that a correct analysis of human nature discloses a love for fellow human creatures which cannot be reduced to self-love.

> To have no restraint from, no regard to others in our behaviour, is the speculative absurdity of considering ourselves as single and independent, as having nothing in our nature which has respect to our fellow-creatures, reduced to action and practice. And this is the same absurdity, as to suppose a hand, or any part to have no natural respect to any other, or to the whole body.[20]

This does not lead to the unrealistic view that man always does good to his fellow creatures, since Butler recognizes the fact of human experience that just as self-love pursued in an unnatural manner leads to injury to the self, so benevolence may be misused. However, in both the case of self-love and benevolence the primary function is to lead to behaviour harmonious to the self as well as to society. In the same manner as "there is no such thing as self-hatred,[21] so neither is there any such thing as ill-

---

[19] *Ibid.*, p. 44, para. 9.

[20] *Ibid.*, p. 45, para. 10.

[21] Sigmund Freud, *New Introductory Lectures on Psycho-analysis* (New York: W. W. Norton & Co., Inc., 1933), pp. 144-5. "It would seem that aggression when it is impeded entails serious injury, and that we have to destroy other things and other people, in order not to destroy ourselves, in order to protect ourselves from the tendency to self-destruction. A sad, disclosure, it will be agreed, for the Moralist.

But the Moralist will, for a long time to come, console himself with the improbability of our speculations."

will in one man towards another".[22] Now although it may be possible to point out specific instances of individuals having a lack of self-love or benevolence, Butler does not consider these negative instances as harmful to his analysis, since his position is based on the great bulk of mankind.

In his first sermon Butler has given his explanation of human nature. In summarizing this development, the highest principle will be discussed first and then the other two in descending order. The category at the peak of the hierarchy of principles is conscience, which has the function of distinguishing between man's actions and approving or disapproving them. The next category is that of self-love and benevolence, the twin principles which regulate man in regard to himself and to society. The third and lowest category is that of the passions, which are innate tendencies of human beings toward certain objects or ends. Some passions are more particularly concerned with self-love and others with benevolence, but all passions are under the jurisdiction of these two principles.

The framework of human nature has now been set up and the next task is to put some content into these distinctions. Butler proceeds to do this in the second and third sermons and to some extent in the remainder of this book. Since his text for Sermon II, Romans 2:14, contains the word "nature", Butler begins by clarifying this concept. "For when the Gentiles, which have not the law, do by nature the things contained in the law, these, having not the law, are a law unto themselves."

Now the word "nature" may be loosely used to refer to any principle in man in the sense that anything within man is a part of his nature. Again, it may mean the strongest principle in man at any given time. However, both of these uses are inadequate for Butler. The writer of Romans meant that there is a divine revelation given to man (the law), which tells man what he should do; however, there are cases (the Gentiles), who act in accordance with the divine revelation without being aware that there is such a thing. How can such a thing happen? The theist answers that the author of special divine revelation has also revealed his

[22] II, Sermon I, p. 46, para. 11.

commandments by other means; this is stated in the following verse, Romans 2:15, which Butler does not include in his text. but which he quotes in the context of this argument. The Gentiles are "a law unto themselves: which show the work of the law written in their hearts, their conscience also bearing witness, and their thoughts the meanwhile accusing or else excusing one another". This is the clew to the proper notion of "nature"; man's conscience has the function of judging and controlling all of the other internal principles. When this principle is in proper control so that all of the other principles are functioning harmoniously, then the proper notion of human nature is obtained.

There is a superior principle of reflection or conscience in every man, which distinguishes between the internal principles of his heart, as well as his external actions: which passes judgment upon himself and them; pronounces determinately some actions to be in themselves just, right, good; others to be in themselves evil, wrong, unjust; which, without being consulted, without being advised with, magisterially exerts itself, and approves or condemns him the doer of them accordingly.[23]

This conscience, which is part of each man's endowment, makes man a moral agent.

If this conception of nature is to be valid, Butler needs to give some evidence for a hierarchy of man's internal principles, and he attempts to do this by means of an illustration. It is considered natural for an animal to satisfy his appetite by following a bait into a trap. However, if a man acted in the same way in a similar situation to satisfy his passion of the moment, it is considered unnatural. Such a judgment is made, according to Butler, by comparing the action to the agent and not by considering the action in itself. Why is such an action considered unnatural for man? If a man acted according to the passion of the moment and entered the trap, he would be acting according to one of his internal principles, or if he acted according to self-love and did not enter the trap, he would also be acting according to another internal principle. Since both of these are internal principles, why is the distinction made by calling the following of passion unnatural and the following of self-love natural? The

[23] II, Sermon II, p. 59, para. 10.

difference cannot be accounted for on the basis of strength or, degree, but must be accounted for by differentiating self-love as different in kind or nature from the passion. If passion prevails over self-love, the action is unnatural; but if self-love prevails over passion, the action is natural. Therefore, if man is to act in conformity with his nature, self-love must govern the passions. "Thus, without particular consideration of conscience, we may have a clear conception of the *superior nature* of one inward principle to another; and see that there really is this natural superiority, quite distinct from degrees of strength and prevalency." [24]

The next logical step would be to show the supremacy of conscience over the other two categories of internal principles; but Butler limits his argument to showing that the conscience is superior to the passions. Passion is defined as a simple, direct tendency towards an object without regard to the means used to attain the object, so it may happen that the object desired by the passion cannot be obtained without injury to another human being. When this is the case, conscience disapproves of the pursuit of this object; but the desire for the object still remains. The question remains: which of these two conflicting internal principles is to be obeyed? Butler's argument is weaker here than when deciding between self-love and the passions, since he just declares that conscience is superior in kind to passion, and if passion should prevail, it is usurpation. But the matter is not left here, since Butler asserts that the notion of authority is part of the very idea of conscience.

Thus that principle, by which we survey, and either approve or disapprove our own heart, temper, and actions, is not only to be considered as what is in its turn to have some influence; what may be said of every passion, of the lowest appetites: but likewise as being superior; as from its very nature manifestly claiming superiority over all others: insomuch that you cannot form a notion of this faculty, conscience without taking in jugdment, direction, superintendency. This is a constituent part of the idea, that is, of the faculty itself: and, to preside and govern, from the very economy and constitution of man, belongs to it. Had it strength, as it has right; had it power, as it has manifest authority; it would absolutely govern the world.[25]

24 *Ibid.*, p. 2, para. 16.
25 *Ibid.*, p. 4, para. 19.

This distinction between power and authority is in harmony with Butler's conception of man as existing in a state of probation in the present life here on earth. It is man's very nature to have his actions influenced by his conscience; but the degree of this influence exercised by the conscience is dependent upon the extent the individual will allow it to function. Therefore, the very concept of the nature of man contains the idea that man has a conscience with the function of exercising authority over the other internal principles. But the power of the conscience depends upon the person and thus varies from individual to individual. Even if the conscience has little or no power, it still has the authority to judge; but its judgements will be ineffectual. The suggestion as to the source of authority of the conscience is found in Butler's notion that it is included in the very idea of man. But man is not an autonomous being; the origin of his being as well as the continued existence of his being depends upon the will of God. God has placed conscience within man to be his proper governor.

This is its right and office: thus sacred is its authority. And how often soever men violate and rebelliously refuse to submit to it, for supposed interest which they cannot otherwise obtain, or for the sake of passion which they cannot otherwise gratify; this makes no alteration as to the *natural right* and *office* of conscience.[26]

God's relationship to man is stated in different terms earlier in this same discussion. In a rather lengthy footnote where he is arguing against Hobbes' position that benevolence can be reduced to the love of power, Butler uses the technique of bringing up instances he holds to be incapable of explanation by Hobbes' theory. "These are the absurdities which even men of capacity run into, when they have occasion to belie their nature, and will perversely disclaim that image of God was originally stamped upon it, the traces of which, however, faint, are plainly discernible upon the mind of man." [27]

It was noted above that Butler did not proceed to argue for the superiority of conscience over the next category in his internal hierarchy, the two principles of self-love and benevolence, but

---

[26] *Ibid.*, pp. 64-5, para. 20.
[27] *Ibid.*, Sermon I, p. 3, fn.

merely argued that the conscience was superior to the passions, the third category. In his definition of conscience, however, he included the idea of authority over the other principles; but no examples were given of the conscience exercising its authority over self-love and benevolence. Although no positive illustration was given, Butler closes the second sermon with an illustration of the consequences that would follow if the conscience did not have authority over the other inward principles, or in other words, he uses a negative case. Suppose someone were guilty of parricide. It is obvious that the passion to kill was the momentary strongest inward principle. If there were no hierarchy of inward principles so that the only criterion between them was strength, there would be no basis for judging this act. There would be no difference in the suitableness of the murder of the father to the nature of man than of an act of filial duty to the nature of man. Both of these cases would have to be approved or disapproved equally, and Butler considers this most absurd.

With this development, Butler considers that the natural supremacy of the conscience has been established and that the next thing to be considered is the formulation of the meaning of "human nature". When this has been accomplished, it will be possible to know what it meant to say that virtue consists in following human nature and vice in deviating from human nature. This is the burden of the third sermon, which is thus a continuation of his discussion of human nature.

In the same manner as the notion of civil government implies the subordination of the various parts to some supreme authority, so the notion of human nature consists of various principles related to each other but subordinated to the superior principle of conscience. "Every bias, instinct, propension within, is a real part of our nature, but not the whole: add to these the superior faculty, whose office it is to adjust, manage, and preside over them, and take in this its natural superiority, and you complete the idea of human nature." [28] Human nature consists of a system of interrelated parts with one part, the conscience, considered as the regulator and controller. Human nature is not only the sum

[28] II, Sermon III, pp. 67-8, para. 1.

of its various parts, but also must contain the relationship between these parts. The body is an organic unity in the same manner as any other living thing. With this established to his satisfaction, Butler is now ready to apply this analysis of human nature to man's actions.

And from all these things put together, nothing can be more evident, than that exclusive of revelation, man cannot be considered as a creature left by his Maker to act at random, and live at large up to the extent of his natural power, as passion, humour, willfulness, happen to carry him; which is the condition brute creatures are in: but that from his make, constitution, or nature, he is in the strictest and most proper sense a law to himself. He hath the rule of right within: what is wanting is only that he honestly attend to it.[29]

The extent that Butler's thought was under the influence of his age can readily be seen from his assertion that apart from revelation man still can determine how he should act. This was one of the primary contentions of the deists; because man could determine how he should act by proper use of his facilities, a separate supernatural revelation was not necessary. Butler agrees that man can have this information apart from revelation; but this does not mean that he is divorcing his ethics from his theistic framework. Although man has this possibility, he may not be using it properly in this state of probation, so God has provided man with a check on his conclusions through the divine revelation that republishes the content of natural revelation. God has given man this ability through creation, and by a special act at later times gave man a means of checking his conclusions.

This gives rise to the optimistic notion that it is within the possibility of every man to determine how he should act. Although it may be a worthwhile activity to inquire after a general rule that would denominate our actions as good or evil, any "plain honest man" [30] who asks himself if his contemplated action is right or wrong will come to the proper conclusion. "I do not in the least doubt, but that this question would be answered agreeably to truth and virtue, by almost any fair man in almost any cir-

[29] *Ibid.*, p. 69, para, 3.
[30] *Ibid.*, p. 70, para. 4.

cumstance." [31] Although Butler does not pursue the implications of the above remarks, it seems fair to say that it might be possible to find some general rule of action for man; but the important thing is the ability of each individual man to determine the rightness or wrongness of the particular action that he is contemplating. The individual may be influenced by superstition or partiality to himself; but compensation can be made for these tendencies. There is a rightness or wrongness to particular actions that can be determined by any individual when he objectively investigates that action.

Granted that the individual is able to determine what is the right course of action in some particular situation, is this individual under any obligation to pursue the right course?

I answer: it has been proved that man by his nature is a law to himself, without the particular distinct consideration of the positive sanctions of that law; the rewards and punishments which we feel, and those from the light of reason we have ground to believe are annexed to it. The question then carries its own answer along with it. Your obligation to obey this law, is its being the law of your nature. That your conscience approves of and attests to such a course of action, is itself alone an obligation. Conscience does not only offer itself to show us the way we should walk in, but it likewise carries its own authority with it, that it is our natural guide; the guide assigned us by the Author of our nature: it therefore belongs to our condition of being, it is our duty to walk in that path, and follow this guide, without looking about to see whether we may not possibly forsake them with impunity.[32]

Man is obligated to follow the dictates of his conscience because he is a law unto himself. In a sense it is meaningless to ask why a man is obligated to follow his conscience. If you accept the analysis that conscience is the highest in the hierarchy of principles, then when you act according to your conscience, you are acting according to your own nature. In other words, conscience performs two functions: (1) it judges the rightness or wrongness of the particular action, and (2) it manifests authority by indicating that the right action should be pursued. God, the author of human

[31] *Ibid.*
[32] *Ibid.*, p. 1, para. 6.

nature as well as the whole realm of experience, has given each man his conscience as a guide to action.

Now this description of the conscience seems to leave out the factor that the conscience is strongly influenced, if not wholly determined, by the individual's culture. Are we therefore free to dismiss this analysis as invalid? If the decision were to be made on the above argument, the answer would most likely be yes; but Butler brings in the factor of social pressure through other means. The society not only classifies acts as virtuous or vicious, but also influences the individual to act virtuously by means of approval or disapproval and reward or punishment. This position has an added advantage. Since the society does not directly influence conscience, the possibility is left open that the conscience may judge as evil some action condoned by society.

Another objection is that of the egoistic hedonist. Why should the individual be concerned about anyone other than himself? The restraints felt by the individual may very well hinder his attaining his own good and should be suppressed. Such an objection has no meaning for Butler because human nature is what it is and because the conditions of the world where the individual has been placed are what they are. The hedonistic position is based on the assumption that the individual's happiness in this world is in no way dependent upon other individuals.

Whereas, on the contrary, the enjoyments, in a manner all the common enjoyments of life, even the pleasures of vice, depend upon these regards of one kind or another to our fellow-creatures. Throw off all regards to others, and we should be quite indifferent to infamy and to honour; there could be no such thing at all as ambition; and scarce any such thing as covetousness; for we should likewise be equally indifferent to the disgrace of poverty, the several neglects and kinds of contempt which accompany this state; and to the reputation of riches, the regard and respect they usually procure. Neither is restraint by any means peculier to one course of life: but our very nature, exclusive of consciensce and our condition, lays us under an absolute necessity of it. We cannot gain any end whatever without being confined to the proper means, which is often the most painful and uneasy confinement. And in numberless instances a present appetite cannot be gratified without such apparent and immediate ruin and misery, that the most dissolute man in the world chooses to forego the pleasure, rather than endure the pain.[33]

On the basis of this development, Butler is able to say that virtue consists in man following his own nature and vice consists in deviating from his nature. This is what the ancient moralists meant by their usage of this concept and what has been commonly felt by men throughout various ages. Man's nature involves the harmonious functioning of all of the different principles in the hierarchy with conscience at the apex. Man is not acting virtuously when some principle other than the conscience is momentarily supreme, which is another manner of saying that a man acts viciously when he acts according to his passions, self-love, or benevolence instead of his conscience. When the complaint is made that the individual is restricted when he cannot follow his passions, the complainer is unwitingly advocating a course of action contrary to his own best interests, since his best interests are in line with acting according to his nature. An individual's happiness does not follow from his pursuing the passions that supposedly lead to his own self-satisfaction, because each individual's happiness is tied up with his relationship to other individuals. It is just a fact of nature that the individual who is acting according to his own best interest is limited to the extent that he cannot possibly pursue all of the desires of his passions. But this does not put the virtuous man at a disadvantage, since the vicious man also finds himself within limits.

Whoever will consider the restraints from fear and shame, the dissimulation, mean arts of concealment, servile compliances, one or other of which belong to almost every course of vice, will soon be convinced that the man of virtue is by no means upon a disadvantage in this respect. How many instances are there in which men feel and own and cry aloud under the chains of vice with which they are enthralled, and which they will not shake off? How many instances, in which persons manifestly go through more pains and self-denial to gratify a vicious passion, than would have been necessary to the conquest of it? To this is to be added, that when virtue is become habitual, when the temper of it is acquired, what was before confinement ceases to be so, by becoming choice and delight. Whatever

[33] *Ibid.*, p. 72, para. 8.

restraint and guard upon ourselves may be needful to unlearn any unnatural distortion or odd gesture; yet, in all propriety of speech, natural behaviour must be the most easy and unrestrained. It is manifest that, in the common course of life, there is seldom any inconsistency between our duty and what is *called* interest: it is much seldomer that there is an inconsistency between duty and what is really our present interest; meaning by interest, happiness and satisfaction.[34]

This implies that self-love and virtue are not contradictory. There is somewhat a problem of terminology because self-love has the connotation of egoistic hedonism. The idea is, rather, that of enlightened self-interest or perhaps the closest one word is "prudence' in the sense of putting wisdom into practical use. The goal of prudence is the happiness of the individual, and this is best obtained by following man's own nature. Because things are the way that they are, when man is doing his duty by following the dictates of his conscience, he is at the same time acting in the manner that will best promote his own happiness. Interest and duty are not inconsistent.

But do interest and duty always coincide in experience? Most everyone would agree that they are in conflict at times; but Butler maintains that the conflicts are fewer than commonly thought.

Self-love, then, though confined to the interest of the present world, does in general perfectly coincide with virtue; and leads us to one and the same course of life. But, whatever exceptions there are to this, which are much fewer than they are commonly thought, all shall be set right at the final distribution of things. It is a manifest absurdity to suppose evil prevailing finally over good, under the conduct and administration of a perfect Mind.[35]

So even in the few instances where self-interest and duty actually do conflict, this is not the final disposition of the situation but only in the present status of life. In the final disposition of things, an event that is in the status following death, God will put all things into their proper order. Such a claim makes sense, only on the basis of his theistic framework.

[34] *Ibid.*, p. 74, para. 11.
[35] *Ibid.*

This leads into a discussion of the relationships that these various principles have to one another within the individual. Before introducing an interpretation that is thought to be the most harmonious with Butler's thought, the traditional interpretations will be discussed. The four principles to be included within any interpretation are the conscience, self-love, benevolence, and the several passions. The problem arises from the fact that Butler is not consistent in listing these principles nor in the relationships they have to one another.

When Butler sets forth the principles in Sermon I, he enumerates all four of the categories listed above in the following order: self-love and benevolence, the several passions and affections, and conscience as the supreme principle. On the basis of this information, the following diagram would describe the hierarchy.

Conscience

Self-love   Benevolence

Several Passions   (Affections-Appetites)

The suggestion is given, although not elaborated with examples, that some of the passions more particularly tend to self-love and other passions to benevolence. But whether or not this is the case, self-love and benevolence are regulatory principles over all of the various passions. The highest and most supreme principle is the conscience, which has the authority, but not always the power, to rule over the other principles. This diagram certainly does justice to the introduction of Butler's analysis of human nature giving a very formal arrangement based on the authority of the various principles. C. D. Broad is an example of an ethical theorist who accepts this interpretation.[36] However, as stated earlier, the basic problem with this interpretation is that Butler does not consistently speak of the principles in this manner. This could be explained by saying this is really what he meant, and at all other times he was using language loosely. The alternative is that when he spoke this way he was using his language

---

[36] C. D. Broad, *op. cit.*, p. 71. "I have assumed throughout that he regards benevolence as a general principle which impels us to maximise the happiness of humanity without regard to persons, just as he regards self-love as a general principle leading us to maximise our own total happiness."

loosely, and he understood the relationship in some other manner.

A diagram for the second traditional interpretation of the hierarchy of principles can be based on the paragraph where Butler summarizes his whole argument on human nature.

The whole argument, which I have been now insisting upon, may be thus summed up, and given you in one view. The nature of man is adapted to some course of action or other. Upon comparing some actions with this nature, they appear suitable and correspondent to it: from comparison of other actions with the same nature, there arises to our view some unsuitableness or disproportion. The correspondence of actions to the nature of the agent renders them natural: their disproportion to it, unnatural. That an action is correspondent to the nature of the agent, does not arise from its being agreeable to the principle which happens to be the strongest: for it may be so, and yet be quite disproportionate to the nature of the agent. The correspondence therefore, or disproportion, arises from somewhat else. This can be nothing but a difference in nature and kind, altogether distinct from strength, between the inward principles. Some then are in nature and kind superior to others. And the correspondence arises from the action being conformable to the higher principle; and the unsuitableness from its being contrary to it. Reasonable self-love and conscience are the chief or superior principles in the nature of man: because an action may be suitable to this nature, though all other principles be violated; but becomes unsuitable, if either of these are. Conscience and self-love, if we understand our true happiness, always lead us the same way. Duty and interest are perfectly coincident; for the most part in this world, but entirely and in every instance if we take in the future, and the whole; this being emplied in the notion of a good and perfect administration of things. Thus they who have been so wise in their generation as to regard only their own supposed interest, at the expense and to the injury of others, shall at last find, that he who has given up all the advantages of the present world, rather than violate his conscience and the relation of life, has infinitely better provided for himself, and secured his own interest and happiness.[37]

If reasonable self-love and conscience are the superior principles, the diagram could be constructed in this manner.[38]

[37] II, Sermon III, pp. 75-6, para. 13.

[38] William J. Norton, *Bishop Butler, Moralist and Divine* (New Brunswick: Rutgers University Press, 1940), pp. 84-5. Norton is not clear on the proper arrangement, but in this passage seems to support this diagram.

Conscience
Self-love
Benevolence
Several Passions

However, if the "and" of the phrase "reasonable self-love and conscience are the chief or superior principles" is taken to mean that they are on the same level, the diagram could be made in either of these two ways; but no interpretors were found who held either of these.

Conscience – Self-love	Conscience and Self-love
Benevolence	Benevolence
Several Passions	Several Passions

The problem with the first interpretation is that in other passages conscience and self-love are regarded as two principles. Its advantage is that it would harmonize with the sentence that preceeds the phrase under consideration where the higher principle is spoken of in the singular. "The correspondence arises from the action being conformable to the higher principle." [39]

Another traditional interpretation, however, introduces another factor because in some passages, the principle of benevolence is used as of it were merely another of the particular passions. Two instances from the preface will be noted. "Benevolence is not more unfriendly to self-love, than any other particular affection whatever." [40] Again, a few paragraphs later, the same type of relationship is noted, "Whoever will consider all the possible respects and relations which any particular affection can have to self-love and private interest, will I think, see demonstrably, that benevolence is not in any respect more at variance with self-love, than any other particular affection whatever, but that it is in every respect, at least, as friendly to it." [41] If this relationship is combined with the suggestion found in the long quote above, the following diagram can be constructed of the second traditional interpretation. Henry Sidgwick is an ex-

[39] II, Sermon III, pp. 75-6, para. 13.
[40] II, *Sermons*, "Preface", p. 29, para. 21.
[41] *Ibid.*, p. 24, para. 32.

ample of an ethical theorist who supports this interpretation.[42]

Conscience and Self-love
Several Passions (Benevolence considered as one of the particular passions)

This general approach has been pushed a little further so that no distinction is seen between conscience and self-love.[43]

Conscience – self-love
Passions (including benevolence)

The main objection to both of these formulations is that it seems to do violence to Butler's long argument on the superior authority of the conscience over all of the other principles, and the fact that the conscience recognizes its own authority. Gladstone adds one of his rather infrequent editorial notes to this passage.

As, in the system of Butler, reasonable self-love is held to be of the nature of virtue, and duty to coincide with interest, there is no direct disparagement to conscience in assigning to it a place by the side of conscience, in respect of superiority to passions and affections. But Butler could hardly mean to predicate of self-love that it was, like conscience, a judicial faculty; or was invested with a like sovereignty.[44]

However, the strong point in favor of this interpretation having conscience and self-love as the superior co-principles comes from its inclusion in Butler's summary of his argument. It would be expected that an author would say what he meant when giving a summary of a long extensive argument.

[42] Henry Sidgwick, *Outlines of the History of Ethics*, 6th Ed. (London: Macmillan & co., Ltd., 1954), p. 195. "There remain, then, Conscience and 'Reasonable Self-love' as the two authorities in the polity of the soul. With regard to these Butler's real views are not (as is widely supposed) that self-love is naturally subordinate to conscience—at least if we consider the theoretical rather than the practical relation between the two. He treats them as independent principles, and so far co-ordinate in authority that it is not 'according to nature' that either should be overruled."

[43] Thomas H. McPherson, "The Development of Bishop Butler's Ethics", Part I, *Philosophy*, Vol. XXIII (Oct. 1948), #87, pp. 326-7. "The fact that Butler used the two terms conscience and cool self-love shows clearly enough that he thought they were distinct principles, but from his own treatment of them in the *Sermons* I hope to show that, although they may be distinguished mentally, they are not to be distinguished in their practical effects. For all practical purposes, conscience *is* cool self-love."

[44] II, "Sermon III", p. 76, fn.

The following suggested interpretation is based on a combination of factors and a reformulation of the components. It includes the suggestion above [45] that the choice of the term "self-love" is unfortunate, since it carries the connotation of egoistic hedonism. The traditional concept of egoistic hedonism is that the individual should pursue his own pleasure exclusively without regard to the pleasure or rights of any other individual; but this is not what Butler meant by self-love. What he did mean was that self-love is the principle within man that strives for that individual's happiness; but because of the very nature of man, he is a social creature, and it is impossible to obtain his own happiness exclusive of the happiness of others. When man is prudent in pursuing his own pleasure, he will find that his own happiness is secured only with due regard to other individuals. When Butler was enumerating the principles within man at the beginning of his discussion, it was necessary to include both self-love and benevolence because of the general usage of these terms. However, after Butler's analysis of the situation, his concept of self-love includes both the older uses of self-love and benevolence, in the sense of prudence. If this development is taken as valid, then the relationships could be diagrammed in this manner.[46]

Conscience
Prudence (includes old meanings of self-love and benevolence)
Passions (including the second meaning of benevolence)

[45] See p. 150 above.
[46] Albert Lefevre, "Self-Love and Benevolence in Butler's Ethical System", Philosophical Review, Vol. IX (March 1900), #2. This diagram is hinted at by Lefevre, but he does not use "prudence". "Self-love must not only have the same end as benevolence, but it must include benevolence, and, to reverse the proposition, benevolence must include self-love. Thus the two become synthesized in one general principle of nature. That Butler recognized, much more clearly than is usually supposed, that they really constitute but one principle is borne out by the statement that merely for purposes of treatment has he abstractly viewed them as separate, since 'there can no comparison be made without considering the things compared as distinct and different'. (Sermon I, para. 3) On account of this methodological dualism, however, one should not, in view of such a caution, which is elsewhere repeated, be led to think that Butler regarded the two principles as distinct faculties or mutually exclusive principles of action.

The advantage of this suggested interpretation is that it preserves the three categories used by Butler to introduce his discussion as well as giving a reason for the omission of benevolence from the summary at the end of Sermon III. It is true that conscience and self-love are the superior principles, since they are included in the top two of the three. The passages that speak of benevolence as a particular passion can be explicated when it is noted that Butler equivocated in his usage of "benevolence" by using it to refer to a principle in one case (which is absorbed in the concept of prudence) and to refer to one of the particular passions in the other case. Both senses of "benevolence" are used in this passage.

> Happiness consists in the gratification of certain affections . . . Love of our neighbor is one of those affections. This, considered as a *virtuous principle*, is gratified by a consciousness of *endeavouring* to promote the good of others; but considered as a natural affection, its gratification consists in the actual accomplishment of this endeavour.[47]

An example of the second case is that of an individual who impulsively acts for the good of another without going through the process of cool rationalization to see if such an action is in his own best interest, although this may well be the case. The busybody in our own society could be said to be acting on the impulse of benevolence.

One quotation used above needs to be brought back into the discussion at this point to show that this is in harmony with Butler's theism. "Self-love then, though confined to the interest of the present world, does in general perfectly coincide with virtue".[48] Now if "prudence" is substituted as suggested, this sentence could be analyzed in this manner. In this present state, the function of prudence (self-love and benevolence) is to pursue the individual's own well-being within the limits of society. When prudence is functioning in the proper manner (i.e., functioning naturally), it is in harmony with the conscience, which judges an

---

They are simply different aspects of reason, which lead to different aspects of the common end of man." Lefevre makes no further elaboration of this point.

[47] II, "Sermon XI", p. 201, para. 16.
[48] II, Sermon III, p. 75, para. 12.

action as virtuous or vicious. This judgment also provides the motive for doing the virtuous action. Prudence, though confined to the present world, coincides with virtue, which is to be pursued as a basis for happiness in the state of existence which follows death. The individual's duty and interest normally coincide, and if for some reason they differ, the individual in such a situation will be pursuing his own interest in the long run if he does his duty in the present life, since "all shall be set right at the final distribution of things".[49]

This section will be closed with a summary of this proposed interpretation of the relationships that Butler theorized were maintained by the principles he found in human nature. Although this interpretation departs somewhat from the traditional interpretations of Butler, it is thought that it gives the better systemization of Butler's thought.

Conscience – Supreme in authority, but not necessarily in power, with the functions of judging an action to be virtuous or vicious and of providing the motivation for doing the virtuous action through this judgment.

Prudence – Limited in sphere of action to the present status of life and combining the more basic concepts of self-love, as egoistic hedonism, and benevolence, as altruism.

Passions – Several in number, one of which is benevolence when such act is done impulsively.

C. TWELVE MORE SERMONS PREACHED AT ROLLS CHAPEL

Although Butler warns in the preface that there is no particular reason for the choice of most of the sermons included in this collection preached over a period of eight years at Rolls Chapel, the position of the first three is important. This can be ascertained from the sub-title to the collection where the sermons "Upon Human Nature" are enumerated separately from the other twelve sermons. The first three summarize Butler's theory of ethics, whereas the following twelve attempt to show how this theory can be put into practice and to elaborate on particular points.

In the development of the sermons, Butler's form of presenta-

[49] *Ibid.*

tion of the constituents of the nature of man represents a return to his position in the first part of the "Preface" and "Sermon I". Self-love and benevolence are given as separate principles that are to control and regulate the passions; the emphasis is placed on the role benevolence should play in the life of man. This emphasis on benevolence is most likely dictated by the temper of the times when Butler was preaching both from the direction of the influence of Hobbes' ethical theory and from the common attitude of the sophisticated of his day who scorned the idea of a "disinterested, generous or public-spirited action".[50] Butler's contention is that there is such a principle of benevolence and that any objective analysis of human nature will come to this conclusion.

The function of self-love and benevolence is to control the passions; but Butler recognizes that the passions are as necessary a part of man's nature as any other of the three categories enumerated. Since they provide the impetus for action, the passions are not be eradicated or suppressed but controlled. In this respect Butler may be compared to Aristotle who held that the passions are necessary but are to be controlled by the reason. In the following passage, for example, Butler clearly makes this distinction between the passions and reason.

It is mankind I am speaking of; imperfect creatures and who naturally depend upon each other. With respect to such creatures, it would be found of as bad consequence to eradicate all natural affections, as to be entirely governed by them. This would almost sink us to the condition of brutes; and that would leave us without a sufficient principle of action. Reason alone, whatever any one may wish, is not in reality a sufficient motive of virtue in such a creature as man; but this reason joined with those affections which God has impressed upon his heart: and when these are allowed scope to exercise themselves but under strict government and direction of reason; then it is we act suitable to our nature, and to the circumstances God has placed us in. Neither is affection itself at all a weakness; nor does it argue defect, any otherwise than as our senses and appetites do; they belong to our condition of nature, and are what we cannot be without.[51]

[50] II, Preface, p. 24, para. 32.
[51] II, Sermon V, p. 98, para. 4.

This passage also points out the similarity of Butler to Aristotle in their commonsense approach to ethical theory and its application in practice. Man has some special nature that makes him what he is, and this nature is to be analyzed in order to find its constituents, the end to which it is adapted, and the circumstances that structure the individual's situation. Butler adds the notion that when this analysis is properly conducted, the theistic framework will provide the explanation. Man is an organism created by God for certain ends and placed within a certain environment, and when this is understood, all of the constituents fall into their proper places.

This analysis will show that man has two principles that are to control his passions: self-love and benevolence. Self-love is the principle that has the man's own good as its primary concern, both in the aspects of fellowmen as individuals and collectively as a unit. Because man is the kind of being he is and because the universe where God has placed man is as it is, self-love and benevolence are not competing as is commonly thought, but rather are supplementary in the sense of prudence.[52] Man is a social creature and his own happiness is dependent upon the happiness of his fellowmen.

Every man is to be considered in two capacities, the private and public; as designed to pursue his own interest, and likewise to contribute to the good of others ... In general there is no contrariety between these; but that from the original constitution of man, and the circumstances he is placed in, they perfectly coincide, and mutually carry each other.[53]

To illustrate how the inward constitution of man is in harmony with the circumstances of man, Butler uses the example of compassion, which is the passion which leads to a course of action to relieve the distressed. It is possible to ignore this passion and pursue one's own interests; but the individual is leaving himself open to some calamity that will humble him. However, when the individual follows the motivation of the passion of compassion, whether in the sense of preventing further distress or relieving

---

[52] See page 150 ff.
[53] II, Sermon V, p. 92, para. 1.

some distress already suffered by another human being, the miseries of life made explicit to him by this act will cause him to have a proper state of mind. The individual is made to think seriously on life and therefore to cultivate the attitudes of moderation, humility, and soberness of mind. By acting in accordance with compassion, the individual is led to reconsider his own place in the whole order of the universe.

The various miseries of life which lie before us where ever we turn our eyes, the frailty of this mortal state we are passing through, may put us in mind that the present world is not our home; that we are merely strangers and travellers in it, as all our fathers were. It is therefore to be considered as a foreign country; in which our poverty and wants, and the insufficient supplies of them, were designed to turn our views to that higher and better state we are heirs to: a state where will be no follies to be overlooked, no miseries to be pitied, no wants to be relieved; where the affection we have been treating of will happily be lost, as there will be no objects to exercise it upon: for 'God shall wipe away all tears from their eyes, and there shall be no more death, neither sorrow, nor crying; neither shall there be any more pain; for the former things are passed away'.[54]

So, by following his innate tendency for compassion toward his fellowmen, man recognizes the state of affairs in this world as they really are and is brought to the point where he begins to think of the next state of human life in accord with the teachings of the Christian religion.

If the proper course of life for man is to analyze his own constitution and environment, why has man not been made less imperfect or placed in a better environment? Such a question Bishop Butler considers out of order. It is taken for granted that a perfectly good deity brought the universe into being, that benevolence is the general law of all moral creation, and that God foresaw the natural and moral disorders which have occurred. But, if man insists on asking why God made the universe as it is and why he did not prevent the disorders which have occurred, then man is usurping his position. These are the wrong questions to ask; the proper questioning procedure is to inquire the end or purpose of the various constituents in human nature that God

[54] II, Sermon VI, p. 120, para. 14.

has given man. These are ethical sermons, and Butler is interested in the practical question of how man is to act. The answer is found by taking "human nature as it is, and the circumstances in which it is placed as they are; and then consider the correspondence between that nature and those circumstances, any particular affection or passion leads us to".[55] Butler raises this problem because even though he assumes that God has made benevolence the general law of moral creation, there is another principle, self-love, which is popularly thought to be contradictory to benevolence.

Butler was positive that every natural passion, which God has given man, is not evil in itself. To follow a passion to the proper extent as determined by the controlling principles is good; but the holding back or exceeding the determined amount is evil. Yet, men do indulge their passions to such an extent that evil results. It could be questioned if a passion such as resentment could be called good. He recognizes that the danger of resentment is excess with the consequences of malice and revenge. In order to explicate the concept of "resentment"; Butler divides it into two kinds: hasty and sudden resentment, which he calls anger, and settled and deliberate resentment, which he calls malice and revenge. "In all these words is usually implied somewhat vicious; somewhat unreasonable as to the occasion of the passions, or immoderate as to the degree or duration of it." [56] This seems to be working against Butler's purpose of trying to show that there is no passion evil in itself, since all of the words he uses to explicate resentment imply viciousness. But if you allow hasty and sudden resentment to be called anger, the way is left upon for Butler to appeal to the New Testament to show that anger is a natural passion and therefore indifferent in itself.

St. Paul has asserted . . . 'Be ye angry, and sin not': which though it is by no means to be understood as an encouragement to indulge ourselves in anger, the sense being certainly this, 'though ye be angry, sin not'; yet here is evidently a distinction made between anger and sin; between the natural passion, and sinful anger.[57]

[55] II, Sermon VIII, p. 136, para. 1.
[56] II, Sermon VIII, pp. 138-9, para. 5.
[57] *Ibid.*, fn Eph. 4 : 26.

Resentment, then, is not evil in itself; Butler then goes on to point out that it is of positive value for the individual. Sudden anger is the passion that is excited by opposition, sudden danger, and violence, and allows the individual to defend himself.

Resentment may also be excited in another manner. Butler uses the illustration of reading a ficticious story of a base and vicious nature. He thinks that the immediate reaction of the reader is that of indignation and desire for punishment. Even if the intended viciousness is prevented, the passion is still raised.

Suppose the story true, this inward feeling would be as natural and as just: and one may venture to affirm, that there is scarce a man in the world, but would have it upon some occasions. It seems *in us* plainly connected with a sense of virtue and vice, of moral good and evil. Suppose further, we knew both the person who did and who suffered the injury: neither would this make any alteration, only that it would probably affect us more. The indignation raised by cruelty and injustice, and the desire of having it punished, which persons unconcerned would feel, is by no means malice. No, it is resentment against vice and wickedness: it is one of the common bonds, by which society is held together; a fellow-feeling which each individual has in behalf of the whole species, as well as of himself. And it does not appear that this, generally speaking, is all too high amongst mankind.[58]

Thus resentment, which at first glance may seem to be evil in itself, is shown by Butler to actually be good in the sense that it is an aid to man. This applies only to the sudden anger aspect and not to the settled malice aspect that Butler distinguishes as the vicious aspect of this passion. The fact is that "every man carries about him this passion, which affords him demonstration, that the rules of justice and equity are to be the guide of his actions . . . for every man naturally feels an indignation upon seeing instances of villainy and baseness, and therefore cannot commit the same without being self-condemned".[59]

The first conclusion that Butler wishes to draw from his discussion of resentment is that vice is of ill desert and that it must finally be punished. The second is that man should be careful in blaming God for the nature he has given man when the blame

[58] *Ibid.*, p. 141, para. 8.
[59] *Ibid.*, p. 149, para. 19.

belongs to the excesses of man's own passions. "Human nature considered as the divine workmanship, should methinks be treated as sacred: for *in the image of God made he man* . . . how manifold evidence have we of the divine wisdom and goodness, when even pain in the natural world, and the passion we have been now considering in the moral [world], come out instances of it!" [60]

In Sermon IX Butler discusses the situation when the individual is on the receiving end of an action which according to the above discussion results in natural and just resentment. The course of action that the individual should follow is given in the sermon title, "Upon the Forgiveness of Injuries." For Butler, the sum total of morals is "that mankind is a community, that we all stand in a relation to each other, that there is a public end and interest of society which each particular is obliged to promote".[61] Since this is the case, the individual is not allowed to take revenge, which would most likely be the impulse after being injured. The gratification of revenge would contradict both the general obligation to benevolence as well as the end for which resentment was originally given to man.

Resentment is not inconsistent with love of neighbor. One may love his enemy, but yet have resentment against him for his injurious behaviour. Resentment becomes malice when it destroys the natural benevolence towards an individual. The command of God to forgive injury prevents this effect. But may not repeated or great injury overcome natural benevolence? The answer is obviously yes; but there is a reason why this should not be the case.

It is not man's being a social creature, much less his being a moral agent, from whence *alone* our obligations to good-will towards him arise. There is an obligation to it prior to either of these, arising from his being a sensible creature; that is, capable of happiness or misery. Now this obligation cannot be superseded by his moral character.[62]

But Butler still has one more reason why man should be for-

---

[60] *Ibid.*
[61] II, Sermon IX, p. 155, para. 7.
[62] *Ibid.*, p. 159, para. 11.

giving in temperament. Suppose yourself as approaching death, and you realize that you are to appear before God as the judge. Could you expect to receive forgiveness if you had been unforgiving during your life? Butler does not think so and uses the parable in Matthew 28 of the king who took account of his servants to support this contention. "So likewise shall my heavenly Father do also unto you, if ye from your hearts forgive not every one his brother their trespasses." [63] On the other hand, if you have been forgiving in life, you can reasonably expect such treatment from God.

'If ye forgive men their trespasses, your heavenly Father will likewise forgive you.' And that we might have a constant sense of it upon our mind, the condition is expressed in our daily prayer. A forgiving spirit is therefore absolutely necessary, as ever we hope for pardon of our own sins, as ever we hope for peace of mind in our dying moments, or for the divine mercy at that day when we shall most stand in need of it.[64]

In Sermons XI and XII, which are perhaps the best known outside of the first three sermons on human nature, Butler discusses in more detail the love of our neighbor. The problem with this discussion is that Butler does not make it clear when he is using love of neighbor in the sense of benevolence as a governing principle or as a particular passion. Since it is often considered that self-love is in opposition to love of neighbor, Butler intends "to inquire what respect benevolence hath to self-love, and the pursuit of private interest to the pursuit of public".[65] Every man has self-love in the sense of a general desire for his own happiness as well as a variety of passions that "together make up that particular nature, according to which man is made".[66] Self-love, which is an ability of all creatures who can reflect upon themselves and their own happiness, pursues an internal object which may be called the individual's happiness, enjoyment, or satisfaction, whether or not this is an explicitly formulated concept. On the other hand, the object of a passion is always a particular

---

[63] *Ibid.*, p. 167, para. 20.
[64] *Ibid.*, para. 21.
[65] II, Sermon XI, p. 186, para. 2.
[66] *Ibid.*, p. 187, para. 3.   . .

external thing itself and not toward the pleasure which arises from it. This follows from Butler's position that there would be no pleasure if it were not for a prior suitableness between the passion and its object.

The principle we call self-love never seeks any thing external for the sake of the thing, but only as a means of happiness or good: particular affections rest in the external thing themselves. One belongs to man as a reasonable creature reflecting upon his own interest or happiness, The other, though quite distinct from reason, are as much a part of human nature.[67]

Self-love is that principle which desires the individual's own happiness, while the passions desire particular external objects.

Since this is the case, happiness is not equivalent to self-love. The desire of a thing is different from the possession of the thing desired. Happiness really consists in the enjoyment of objects which by nature are suited to man's passions. "Self-love then does not constitute *this* or *that* to be our interest or good; but, our interest or good being constituted by nature . . . self-love only puts us upon obtaining and securing it." [68] In the same manner as self-love is a regard to the individual's own good, so benevolence is a regard to the good of mankind. Benevolence here seems to be used in the sense of a regulating principle; but a little further on in his sermon, Butler seems to consider benevolence as one of the particular passions.[69] "Thus it appears that there is not peculiar contrariety between self-love and benevolence; no greater competition between these, than between any other particular affections and self-love." [70] Even though it is recognized that Butler equivocated in his usage of "benevolence", in this passage he seemingly is using it in the sense of a principle but putting it into a class with the other particular passions as both being distinct from self-love. In order to harmonize this passage with the position that self-love and benevolence are principles distinct from the passions, it could be suggested that this is a part of Butler's sermonic technique in persuading his

[67] *Ibid.*
[68] *Ibid.*, p. 190, para. 6.
[69] See pp. 151 ff. above.
[70] II, Sermon XI, p. 196, para. 11.

audience that there is really no conflict between self-love and benevolence. After his introduction, Butler begins with a discussion of the difference between self-love and the passions and then later benevolence is introduced into the discourse. In pounding home his point, it would be quite natural to argue that just as there is no real conflict between self-love and the various passions, so there is no real conflict between self-love and this newly introduced idea of benevolence. This is based on Butler's suggestion, "let us now see whether there be any peculiar contrariety between the respective courses of life which these affections lead to; whether there be any greater competition between the pursuit of private and public good, than between any other particular pursuits and that of private good".[71]

This confusion and inconsistent use of terms continues as Butler leads to the most controversial paragraph in his *Sermons.* The passage begins with the assertion that even religion, from which arises the strongest obligation to benevolence, appeals to self-love in order to convince men that the religious life is not really contrary to their own interest. It may be that the individual's ideas of happiness and misery are the closest to him; but there should never be any inconsistency between them and other principles such as order, beauty, harmony, and proportion. Then the controversial statement appears.

> Let it be allowed, though virtue of moral rectitude does indeed consist in affection to the pursuit of what is right and good as such; yet, that when we sit down in a cool hour, we can neither justify to ourselves this or any other pursuit, till we are convinced that it will be for our happiness, or at least not contrary to it.[72]

What is Butler doing here? Is he after all his arguing merely an egoistic hedonist? Even though virtue consists in pursuing right and the good as such, yet this pursuit must be justified in terms of self-interest. If this passage is taken at face value, it sets aside the remainder of Butler's writings.

Because of this implication, attempts have been made to harmonize this passage with the intent of Butler's position. S. A.

[71] *Ibid.*
[72] *Ibid.*, p. 206, para. 21.

Grove lists at least three different attempts that have been made to show that this sentence cannot be taken as it stands by itself.[73] (1) Butler in this particular sermon is appealing to self-love, since he recognizes it as the favorite passion of his audience. This is supported by his declaration near the beginning of the sermon: "These inquiries, it is hoped, may be favourably attended to: for there shall be all possible concessions made to the favourite passion, which hath so much allowed to it, and whose cause is universally pleaded: it shall be treated with the utmost concern for its interests." [74] Since Butler has argued in so many instances that there is no conflict between virtue and self-love,[75] he is really making no concession to self-love but is merely appealing to his audience.

(2) Because of the introductory phrase at the beginning of this sentence, this may not be Butler's position at all, but a hypothetical position that he is using. The "let it be allowed" may infer an impersonal statement of a position without committing himself to this particular position. The point at the beginning of this paragraph is that religion appeals to men on the basis of self-interest. Then Butler uses two concessive arguments with the first one introduced by "it may be allowed" and the second concessive argument "let it be allowed". This explanation takes the two sentences to be parallel. In order to make this position clearer, the first concessive argument is given.

It may be allowed, without any prejudice to the cause of virtue and religion, that our ideas of happiness and misery are of all our ideas the nearest and the most important to us; that they will, nay, if you please, that they ought to prevail over those of order, and beauty, and harmony, and proportion, if there should ever be, as it is impossible there ever should be, any inconsistence between them: though these last too, as expressing the fitness of actions are real as truth itself.[76]

The sentence under consideration immediately follows this sentence.

[73] S. A. Grove, "The Foundation of Butler's Ethics", *The Australasian Journal of Philosophy and Psychology*, Vol. XXX (Aug. 1952), #2, p. 83.

[74] II, Serman XI, p. 186, para. 2.

[75] Subject of Sermon XII.

[76] II, Sermon XI, p. 206, para. 21.

(3) Butler in this passage is using a technique that he explicitly states in the second part of the *Analogy* as arguing "upon the principles of others, not my own".[77] He, of course, does not mean that he is basing his arguments on the premises of others, but that arguments based on the premises of others do not invalidate his assertions. In this particular case he is arguing that even if you do give self-love the primary place, this does not mean that self-love and benevolence are opposed. Benevolence, in the sense of love of neighbor, is the subject of this sermon, and he is driving home the point that self-love is not in conflict with benevolence.

The concluding paragraph of this sermon gives evidence that Butler is not, after all, an egoistic hedonist, but maintains an element of duty in his ethics. The fact is that "Christianity lays us under new obligations to a good life, as by it the will of God is more clearly revealed, and as it affords additional motives to the practice of it, over and above those which arise out of the nature of virtue and vice; I might add, as our Saviour has set us a perfect example of goodness in our own nature".[78] Here is the answer to the question, what is man to do? He is to lead a good life. Motives for the individual to lead a good life are enumerated: (1) Christianity reveals that God's will for man is that the individual should live a good life, (2) the nature of virtue and vice are such that man should pursue virtue and abhor vice, and (3) the example which Jesus set as a good man. From the context of this sermon, the additional motive of self-interest may be added, since it is in harmony with the good life. The characteristics of the good life are not discussed; but Butler assumed them to be those commonly held by the society of his day and these characteristics would be in harmony with those recognized by men of all times and all places.[79]

Sermon XII, the second sermon on love of our neighbors, brings out the meaning of benevolence (which is the equivalent of charity, good-will, or love or neighbor)[80] as Sermon XI was

[77] I, *Analogy*, Part II, chap. 8, p. 267, para. 23.
[78] II, "Sermon XI", p. 207, para. 23.
[79] See p. 97 above. Butler held that there was such agreement.
[80] II, "Sermon XII", p. 209, para. 2.

an exposition of self-love. Butler uses Romans 13:9 as his text: "And if there be any other commandment, it is briefly comprehended in this saying, namely, thou shalt love thy neighbor as thyself." Benevolence is "an affection to the good and happiness of our fellow-creature. This implies in it a disposition to produce happiness: and this is the simple notion of goodness, which appears so amiable wherever we meet with it".[81] This is the closest that Butler has come to Utilitarianism; [82] but in other places he notes that this is not the whole of virtue, which he seems to use as interchangeable with good.

What does it mean to love our neighbor as ourself?

First, the precept may be understood as requiring only, that we have the *same kind* of affection to our fellow-creatures, as to ourselves, which disposes him to avoid misery, and consult his own happiness; so we should cultivate the affection of good-will to our neighbor, and that it should influence us to have the same kind of regard to him. This at least must be commanded: and this will not only prevent our being injurious to him, but will also put us upon promoting his good. There are blessings in life, which we share in common with others; peace, plenty, freedom, healthful seasons. But real benevolence to our fellow-creatures would give us the notion of a common interest in a stricter sense: for in the degree we love another, his interest, his joys and sorrows, are our own. It is from self-love that we form the notion of private good, and consider it as our own: love of our neighbor would teach us thus to appropriate to ourselves his good and welfare; to consider ourselves as having a real share in his happiness ... Thus, as the private affection makes us in a peculiar manner sensible to humanity, justice, or injustice, when exercised towards ourselves; love of our neighbor would give us the same kind of sensibility in his behalf. This would be the greatest security of our uniform obedience to that most equitable rule; 'whatsoever ye would that men should do to you, do ye even so to them'.[83]

Butler maintains, then, that love of neighbor means that we have the same kind of love to others as we have to ourselves. We will feel the same way towards others as we do to ourselves in regard to the *kind* of feelings. But so far, nothing has been said about the *amount* of the feeling in the sense that we should love others

[81] *Ibid.*, pp. 209-10, para. 2.
[82] See p. 69 above.
[83] II, "Sermon XII", pp. 212-3, para. 4.

half, three quarters, or equally as much as we love ourselves. The question now under consideration is how much should we love others?

Secondly, the precept before us may be understood to require, that we love our neighbor in the same certain *proportion* or other, *according as* we love ourselves. And indeed a man's character cannot be determined by the love he bears to his neighbor, considered absolutely: but the proportion which this bears to self-love, whether it be attended to or not, is the chief thing which forms the character, and influences the actions. For, as the form of the body is a composition of various parts; so likewise our inward structure is not simple or uniform, but a composition of various passions, appetites, affections, together with rationality; including in this last both the discernment of what is right, and a disposition to regulate ourselves with it.[84]

This last phrase is of interest because it indicates Butler's close affinity with a rational approach to ethics in particular to Clarke. Rationality discerns what is right and gives the disposition to do what is right.

Butler emphasizes the point brought out in the above quotation that a man's character is dependent upon the relationship between the various internal principles and not by considering each principle in itself. This supports his assertion in the first three sermons that there is a hierarchy of principles within the individual with each of the components acting in harmony. "Now the proportion which the two general affections, benevolence and self-love, bear to each other . . . denominates man's character as to virtue."[85] The implication of the assertion that the individual is to have an equal *amount* of love for others as of self-love seems to be that we would have equal interest for others as for ourself; but according to Butler, this does not follow. Besides the two principles of benevolence and self-love, the individual also has all of his particular passions "which he could not possibly feel in common both for himself and others".[86]

In these two sermons on love of our neighbor Butler first expounded his conception of self-love and then secondly of

---

[84] *Ibid.*, p. 213, para. 5.
[85] *Ibid.*, p. 218, para. 10.
[86] *Ibid.*, p. 228, para. 23.

benevolence. The next two sermons deal with love of God and holds that it is an essential part of an individual's character.

Human nature is so constituted, that every good affection implies the love of itself; i.e. becomes the object of a new affection in the same person. Thus, to be righteous, implies in it the love or righteousness; to be benevolent, the love of benevolence; to be good, the love of goodness; whether this righteousness, benevolence, or goodness, be viewed as in our own mind, or in another's: and the love of God as a being perfectly good, is the love of perfect goodness contemplated in a being or person. Thus morality and religion, virtue and piety, will at last necessarily coincide, run up into one and the same point, and *love* will be in all senses *the end of the commandment.*[87]

The next question to be asked is, what is piety? Butler answers, "resignation to the will of God is the whole of piety: it includes in it all that is good, and is a source of the most settled quiet and composure of mind".[88] Resignation has a healthy effect upon the individual. When the individual realizes that the course of nature cannot be altered and that the individual should be satisfied with his situation, his mind will be quieted. "But when we can add, that this unalterable course is appointed and continued by infinite wisdom and goodness; how absolute should be our trust and dependence!" [89] Resignation to the will of God is faith, honesty, and fairness of mind expanded to a greater extent than is usually done as a response to what God's superior nature requires from man. The outward expression of this is religious worship, which takes the attention from the world that God has made to God himself. This is proper because of the relationship that man has to God.

But if you can lay side that general, confused undeterminate notion of happiness, as consisting in such possessions; and fix in you thoughts, that it really can consist in nothing but in a faculty's having its proper object; you will clearly see, that in the coolest way of consideration, without either the heat of fanciful enthusiasm, or the warmth of real devotion, nothing is more certain, than that an infinite Being may himself be, if he pleases, the supply of all the capacities of our nature. All the common enjoyments of life are from the faculties he hath

---

[87] *Ibid.*, p. 228, para. 23.
[88] II, "Sermon XIV", p. 244, para. 3.
[89] *Ibid.*, p. 246, para. 5.

endued us with, and the objects he hath made suitable to them. He may himself be to us infinitely more than all these: he may be to us all that we want . . . since the supreme Mind, the Author and Cause of all things, is the highest possible object to himself, he may be an adequate supply to all the faculties of our souls.[90]

In the fifteentth and last sermon Butler preaches on a subject he has alluded to several times throughout his works – the ignorance of man. Man can know something of the world in which he lives and of the providence of God; but because the universe is unlimited in extent and duration, the general system is beyond the comprehension of man. This limitation is also emphasized by the fact that "there appears such a subordination and reference of the several parts to each other, as to constitute it properly one administration or government; we cannot have a thorough knowledge of any part, without knowing the whole".[91] The obvious implication is that man should be cautions in judging the small part of the world within his personal limits, since he really does not know the part until he knows the whole. One example from the *Analogy* where Butler uses this type of argument occurs when he cautions those who said that God should have made man and the universe differently, if God intended man to be happy. Butler's reply is that we have no grounds for this criticism from our limited perspective, since the way God did create may very well be the best way for man to be happy. Man's knowledge is limited by the very fact that he is a finite creature.

What are the implications from this assertion that man is ignorant to a certain extent? Butler's first implication is that man cannot expect perfect knowledge in religion when it is not available to him in any other area. If a man has to go on a journey at twilight or in the darkness, he may wish for the sunlight so that he might see the surrounding countryside; but he will use what light is available to him.

If the make and constitution of man, the circumstances he is placed in, or the reason of things affords the least hint or intimation, that virtue is the law he is born under: scepticism itself should lead him to the most strict and inviolable practice of it; that he may not make

90 *Ibid.*, pp. 250-1, para. 12.
91 II, Sermon XV, p. 262, para. 4.

the dreadful experiment, of leaving the course of life marked out for him by nature, whatever that nature be, and entering paths of his own, of which he can know neither the dangers nor the end.[92]

In fact, Butler maintains that knowledge as such is not the proper end of man.

The only knowledge, which is of any avail to us, is that which teaches us our duty, or assists us in the discharge of it. The economy of the universe, the course of nature, almighty power exerted in the creation and government of the world, is out of our reach . . . Our province is virtue and religion, life and manners; the science of improving the temper, and making the heart better. This is the field assigned us to cultivate . . . Virtue is demonstrably the happiness of man: it consists in good actions, proceeding from a good principle, temper, or heart. Overt acts are entirely in our power. What remains is, that we learn to *keep our heart*; to govern and regulate our passions, mind, affections: that so we may be free from the impotencies of fear, envy, malice, covetousness, ambition; that we may be clear of these, considered as vices seated in the heart, considered as constituting a general wrong temper; from which general wrong frame of mind, all the mistaken pursuits, and far the greatest part of the unhappiness of life, proceed. He, who should find out one rule to assist us in this work, would deserve infinitely better of mankind, than all the improvers of other knowledge put together.[93]

D. PUBLIC SERMONS

Because of his position as a bishop, from time to time Butler preached at special meetings of various kinds. Six of these public sermons have been preserved. They will now be summarized and analyzed in the same manner as the other writings of Butler in order to bring out their teaching regarding ethics and theism.

The first public sermon was preached before an anniversary meeting of the Society for the Propagation of the Gospel in Foreign Parts. It contains Butler's clearest statement of his conception of the history of revelation. The general doctrine of religion "that all things are under the direction of one righteous

---

[92] *Ibid.*, p. 268, para. 11.
[93] *Ibid.*, pp. 271-3, paras. 14-5.

Governor" [94] was repeatedly revealed to the first ages of man. It was up to them to either preserve this revelation in its pure and complete form, or to carelessly forget it, or to willfully corrupt it. "And though reason, almost intuitively, bare witness to the truth of this moral system of nature, yet it soon appeared, that 'they did not like to retain God in their knowledge', as to any purposes of real piety." [95] Gradually this natural revelation became corrupted.

Although it was possible by reason to revive natural religion, reason was not able to discover the most important part of the scheme of the world which was Jesus Christ as the mediator. God in his infinite wisdom again chose to reveal in its pure form the information contained in natural religion as well as this new information which is the heart of Christianity. This new revelation is preserved through the Christian church and in its written form in the Christian scriptures. So God has provided many witnesses to man even if, for the most part, they are not regarded: the visible constitution and course of nature, the moral law written upon man's heart, and the positive institutions of religion.

If God had so desired, he could have revealed all religious truth to each individual man. But God did not do so, and it is the duty of those who know to instruct the ignorant.

The same reasons which make it our duty to instruct the ignorant in the relation, which the light of nature shows they stand in to God their maker, and in the obligations of obedience, resignation, and love to him, which arise out of that relation; make it our duty likewise to instruct them in all those other relations, which revelation informs us of, and in the obligations of duty, which arise out of them.[96]

Due to the nature of the occasion where he was speaking, Butler's main point is that all Christians should be active in missionary activity in order to start new churches in unchristian lands as witnesses to these obligations.

This distinction between the content of natural and special revelation brings up an important problem for Butler. In the

[94] II, "Public Sermon I", p. 277, para. 1.
[95] *Ibid.*
[96] *Ibid.*, p. 284, para. 9.

first part of the *Analogy* Butler maintains that man is in a state of probation for the future life in that his actions in this life will determine to a great extent his happiness (or lack of happiness) in the next life. Does this happiness depend, then, upon the obligations of natural revelation or upon special revelation (which also includes natural revelation)? If Butler would take the alternative that future happiness depends upon the obligations of natural religion, then he would be right back with the deists. In this case there woud be no need for a special revelation. Butler's own insistence on the fact that the general run of mankind knows what should be done in particular situations would support this contention, unless he is restricting the idea of general mankind to societies based on Christianity. However, Butler is writing against the deists in the *Analogy,* and his contention is that special revelation is necessary and that there is no good reason for rejecting special revelation if one accepts natural revelation. If Butler takes the second alternative, which is his choice beyond all reasonable doubt, then he falls short of ever establishing why special revelation is not superfluous. If happiness in this life as well as the next life are the goals of man, and man can find out how he is to act through natural revelation, what is the need of special revelation? Of course, special revelation aids with an authoritative republishing of the corrupted original content of natural revelation; but this does not justify the addition of more obligations unknown to natural revelation.

The second public sermon was preached before the Corporation of the City of London on behalf of financial support for various charities. Butler here notes the stratification of society into three levels: the rich, the middle class, and the poor. It is the obligation of the first two classes, especially the rich, to aid the needy poor. In the end, man's charity towards the poor may be exalted into piety toward God from the consideration that we are his creatures. "To relieve the poor *for God's sake*, is to do it in conformity to the order of nature, and to his will, and his example, who is the Author and Governor of it; and in thankful remembrance, that all we have is from his bounty." [97]

[97] II, "Public Sermon II", p. 316, para. 21.

The third public sermon was preached before the House of Lords in the Abbey-Church of Westminster and is a discourse against hypocrisy in government as well as in private life. Since each individual is a servant of God, he should be reminded that he is accountable to God, even if he is out of the reach of all human authority. Human government is not perfect and cannot be expected to cover every situation; but God knows the secret things and will judge every action as to whether it is good or evil.

An appeal to support the charity-schools for needy children was the subject of his fourth public sermon. Butler maintained that the education of children was the duty of society, since a young child is to be trained in the way that he is to live. "Children have as much right to some proper education, as to have their lives preserved; and that when this is not given them by their parents, the care of it devolves upon all persons, it becomes the duty of all, who are capable of contributing to it, and whose help is wanted." [98] Although Butler noted that his viewpoint might be too idealistic, he thought that "upon the whole, incapacity and ignorance must be favourable to error and vice; and knowledge and improvement contribute, in due time, to the destruction of impiety as well as superstition, and to the general prevalence of true religion". [99]

Although the poor children are to be educated as means to furthering their moral improvement, Butler was not advocating a program which would change the class stratification of his day. He notes that care should be taken so as not to set the poor children "above their rank". [100] This echoes a passage in the first public sermon where Butler speaks of slaves as members of the colonies even though inferior members, "and therefore to be treated as members of them; and not merely as cattle or goods, the property of their masters". [101] Butler is for the betterment of people, but within the state of life in which they find themselves.

The fifth public sermon is another preached before the House

---

[98] II, Public Sermon V, p. 341, para. 4.
[99] *Ibid.*, p. 352, para. 18.
[100] *Ibid.*, para. 19.
[101] II, "Public Sermon I", p. 286, para. 12.

of Lords on the anniversary of the king's accession to the throne. The theme is that the aim of man given him in the providence of God is "to lead a quiet and peaceable life, in all godliness and honesty . . . [and this] is the whole that we have any reason to be concerned for. To this the constitution of our nature carries us; and our external condition is adapted to it." [102] Civil government has been instituted in order to help man achieve this end. In fact Butler makes "no scruple to affirm, that civil government has been, in all ages, a standing publication of the law of nature, and an enforcement of it; though never in its perfection, for the most part greatly corrupted, and I suppose always so in some degree".[103] Civil government is that part of God's government over the world which is exercised through the instrumentality of men. As a good Englishman, Butler thinks that the advantages of government are best enjoyed under the form practiced in England.

In his praise of the government including the state-church relationship, Butler makes some of his strongest denouncements of Roman Catholicism, as is mentioned in Chapter III above. Butler was against the Roman Catholic use of persecution in lands where it was in control, and notes that it was an enemy to the Church of England. Butler is appreciative of the outward worship in England and emphasizes this aspect; but he also emphasizes that inward religion must be cultivated.

The last public sermon, the sixth, was preached before the Governors of the London Infirmary, and again Butler is advocating the care of the poor and needy. Butler feared that in the commercialization of his day, the needs of the poor were being overlooked. Butler insists that as not one of his hearers would fail to provide care for a house servant who fell ill, so they should also see their wider responsibility to the poor of the city who in a sense are still servants because of the work that they perform, although removed from the direct supervision of masters because of the growth of society. Because of the fact man owes all of his faculties and the power to exercise them as well as his

---

[102] II, "Public Sermon V", p. 361, para. 1.
[103] *Ibid.*, p. 362, para. 2.

being to God, and as such is not his own, he should be merciful
to his fellowmen. Man is to treat others as he wishes to be treated
at the time of final judgment.

One other public address of Butler's has been preserved, which
was preached as "A Charge to the Clergy" when he became
Bishop of Durham. It was meant as a "pep talk", since Butler
was still dismayed in 1751 over the general decay of religion
which he had mentioned earlier in 1736 in the "Advertisement"
to the *Analogy*. His charge to the clergy is that they should seek
to revive this declining spirit of religion. One means of doing
this is to argue for the defense of religion from the pulpit.

The proof of the being of God, from final causes, or the design and
wisdom which appears in every part of nature; together with the law
of virtue written upon our hearts: the proof of Christianity from
miracles, and the accomplishment of prophecies; and the confirmation
which the natural and civil history of the world give to the scripture
account of things: these evidences of religion might properly be
insisted on, in a way to affect and influence the heart.[104]

Another way to revive religion is to emphasize the form of religion in order to keep it constantly before the minds of people.
This suggestion was discussed in Chapter III above, since it
brought the charge of popery on Butler. Although the reformers
reduced outward religion to a minimum, Butler thought that it
had been neglected. In this charge Butler also advocated one of
his pet projects – the maintenance of church property.

This concludes the study of the published works of Butler.
The last section on his public sermons does not add anything to
the main argument of the *Analogy* and *Sermons,* but rather
emphasizes a point which will help to clarify his thought. Because
man is a creature created by God, man has certain obligation to
his fellowmen, similar creatures created by God. Although seemingly it is theoretically possible for all men to know how they
are to act, this information is not widespread among the heathen
nor among the poor in England, and thus it is the obligation of
those who know (the rich and the middle class) to share this
information. The outward working of benevolence seems to be

[104] II, "Charge", p. 404, para. 11.

channeled through the class structure of eighteenth century England, although it seems implicit in Butler's thought that personal charity is best. However, due to the growth of society, dehumanized charity through institutions seems to be the only way of accomplishing this task.

VII

CONCLUSION

The study of Butler's writings has now been completed, and the time has come to summarize the argument and to discuss some of the implications. The focus of attention has been on the question whether or not Butler as an ethical theorist is necessarily related to Butler as a theistic theologian. The procedure followed has been discussed in Chapter I as the proper method of studying a philosopher. The first part consists of a study of the individual (Chapter II), and it was found that Butler lived the rather uneventful life of an eighteenth century churchman. His activity as a writer was subservient to and fitted into his busy life as a preacher and church administrator.

The next part undertook the discussion of the intellectual framework of the age in which he lived, concentrating on theology (Chapter III) and ethics (Chapter IV). Butler contributed little to the theological thought of his day; in fact, it was difficult to ascertain his opinion on the few subjects of controversy that were under discussion. This might have been due to the religious tone of the age which Broad describes as follows: "the Christian religion was then going through one of its recurrent phases of dormancy, and has seldom been at a lower ebb in England ... Religion was in a resting stage, worn out with the theological excitements of the seventeenth century and awaiting the revival which was to take place in the latter part of the eighteenth." [1] The intellectual approach to religion with almost total disregard for the emotional aspect is exemplified in deism. Although But-

---

[1] C. D. Broad, *Five Types of Ethical Theory* (New York: Harcourt, Brace & Co., 1930), pp. 53-4.

ler's *Analogy* was written in reaction to deism, he had no quarrel with this intellectual approach, but even used an approach parallel to deism in the first part of the *Analogy*. His quarrel with deism was over the fact that they totally disregarded the Christian special revelation in the Old and New Testaments, which Butler considered essential to Christianity. This overemphasis on the intellectual aspects of religion led to the revivals in the second half of the eighteenth century; Butler became acquainted with this movement mainly through the work of Wesley who preached in Bishop Butler's diocese and who was called on the bishop's carpet for this activity.

The ethics of Butler's day was discussed in the framework of reaction mainly to Hobbes and perhaps to some extent to Mandeville. The first reaction was that of the Cambridge Platonists who emphasized the unchangeable permanent essence of things. Cudworth and More argued this way because they interpreted Hobbes as basing ethics on the arbitrary will of God or a sovereign, whereas they contended that a thing is good or evil by nature and is not affected by will. God may create or destroy a thing; but he cannot change the nature of the thing.

The second reaction was from the natural law moralists who contended that there were laws which should govern human conduct in much the same manner as there are laws which govern the conduct of material things. These laws have been established by God and can be ascertained by the individual when he properly exercises his God-given faculty of reason. The individual in no sense creates the laws, but merely discovers these objective laws that exist whether or not anyone recognizes them.

The third approach was that of Clarke and Wollaston, and for want of a better name, they have been called simply the rationalists. Their emphasis is on the relations that things maintain to each other in much the same manner as the Cambridge Platonists emphasized the essence of things. By his use of reason, man is able to ascertain the fitness or unfitness of things. God always acts in accordance with the best fitness of things, and man should attempt to do the same thing to the extent of his limited ability.

The fourth and last school presented in the discussion of the ethical background of Butler was that of the moral sense ethical theorists. Shaftesbury and Hutcheson maintained that man had a special moral sense that enabled him to know how he should act. Shaftesbury was interested in separating ethics from religion; but Hutcheson maintained that the moral sense was God given. The function of this moral sense was more akin to an emotion of the heart than to reason; good and evil were felt rather than rationally apprehended.

This discussion of the ethics in Chapter IV has given a general introduction to the thought patterns of the intelligentsia of Butler's age. They would agree, although the question was not raised in their day, that ethics was a legitimate study. There was a certain manner of action for man which was proper for him, and he could find this way of life by the proper functioning of his native abilities. Most of these philosophers also had a prominent place for God in their ethical systems. This consensus on the existence of God enabled Butler to assume the existence of God in his writing of the *Analogy*.

The third part of an interpretation of a philosopher is a systematic study of his writings. Although this study should be critical, it also should be sympathetic with the author's purpose for writing and with the method he used to accomplish this purpose. The *Analogy* is a closely reasoned argument in defense of Christianity whereas the *Sermons* is a random collection of discourses for the most part delivered over a period of years in Rolls Chapel. Although the *Sermons* are more widely read at the present time (for their ethical content and not as sermons), the *Analogy* really has a wider appeal, since it only assumes the existence of God and the ability of human reason, and then plunges in to argue for the remainder of Christian theism. The fifteen *Sermons* originally had a more particular appeal, since they were preached within the framework of the unity between priest and his parishioners. This relationship was ably summarized above in chapter VI by A. E. Taylor.[2]

Chapter V is a study of the *Analogy* with a concentration on

[2] See page 137.

the first part concerning natural religion and with a brief summary of the second part, which is an argument for Christianity. Throughout both Chapter V on the *Analogy* and Chapter VI on the *Sermons* the attempt has been made to stay rather closely to the actual text of Butler so that the development would reflect how Butler actually philosophized rather than how he would philosophize on certain questions that he had no reason to consider. About the only major divergence from this procedure was in the attempt to reconstruct his theory of the hierarchy of principles within human nature.

In Chapter I, the introduction to this study, it was noted that there are three basic tenets of theism. (1) There is a God. (2) The human individual is immortal. (3) Life in the future state of existence is to some extent dependent upon the individual's conduct in the present state. As was noted above, Butler assumes the existence of God, and then in the remainder of the first part of the *Analogy* he argues for the second two points. The second part of the *Analogy* deals with Christianity and emphasizes the point that the Christian special revelation is a republication of the information that can be known through natural revelation plus the disclosing of information which cannot be known by any other means. This additional information provides the basis for Christianity.

Chapter VI is a study of the *Sermons*. In the Preface and in the first three sermons Butler lays down his thesis that man should live according to his nature. This necessitates an investigation to uncover the components of human nature as well as the relations existing between these components. Butler finds four kinds of components in man: the principle of conscience, the principle of self-love, the principle of benevolence, and the passions. This much is fairly clear; but when Butler turns to a discussion of the relationship among these components, the results are confused. An attempt was made in Chapter VI to summarize the various relationships that have been pointed out by commentators and then to reconstruct a relationship that would follow what Butler was trying to say. The remaining twelve sermons discuss and elaborate points brought up in the first three sermons and the Preface. A few miscellaneous remarks are made about the public sermons in order that all of Butler's writings may be included in this study.

No one questions that Butler was a theist as far as his theology is concerned, but such agreement does not exist in regard to his ethics. It is contended that Butler's ethical development can be separated from his theology not only for the purpose of study, but because there is no basic unity between his theology and ethics. The conclusion reached in this study is that Butler's ethic grew out of his theology, and therefore, they are harmonious. Two different questions, the relationship of duty and interest and the place of man in the universe, will be discussed in support of this contention.

That Butler was trying to maintain the coincidence of interest and duty can be seen from the following passage.

It is manifest that, in the common course of life, there is seldom any inconsistency between our duty and what is *called* interest; it is much seldomer that there is an inconsistency between duty and what is really our present interest; meaning by interest, happiness and satis-faction.

Self-love then, though confined to the interest of the present world, does in general perfectly coincide with virtue; and leads us to one and the same course of life. But, whatever exceptions there are to this, which are much fewer than they are commonly thought, all shall be set right at the final distribution of things. It is a manifest absurdity to suppose evil prevailing finally over good, under the conduct and administration of a perfect Mind.[3]

This idea is not restricted to a few passages, but pervades his whole thinking. When man is following his real interest, he is at the same time following his duty, and, of course, it is man's duty to live virtuously. There is nothing unusual in this for a theist since, as Taylor points out, "Butler, like all Christians, holds that virtue in the end always coincides with interest".[4] Prichard [5] includes Butler along with Plato and Green as examples of philosophers who held that there was a necessary connection between duty and interest. Prichard considers this activity a

---

[3] II, "Sermon III", pp. 74-5, paras. 11-2.

[4] Taylor, *op. cit.*, p. 322.

[5] H. A. Prichard, *Duty and Interest* (Oxford: University Press, 1928).

mistake; but at least he agrees that Butler was engaged in it.

Butler would have no grounds for asserting that interest was coincident with duty, if it were not for his theistic belief in immortality. He readily admits in the above quotation that in the present state of existence there are exceptions to the coincidence of duty and interest, although they may not be as numerous as commonly thought. The point is that only *one* exception would destroy the coincidence between interest and duty. The only way of maintaining this thesis which is contrary to the facts of experience in this life is to hold that this will be the situation in the final distribution of things. The theistic belief is essential to the belief in the coincidence of duty and interest.

The second question concerns man's place in the universe. Butler's conception is that at some time in the past, God created the universe and placed men in it. Man and his environment were so arranged by God that man was at home in his environment. Butler believes this to be an accurate description of the facts of life, and therefore part of the given experience which he must consider. Many questions could be asked about the when, why, how, *et cetera* of creation and especially man's creation; but Butler has limited information on these questions and is thus relatively unconcerned with them. He accepts things as they are and attempts to build from there.

To indicate that this is following Butler's thought, the following quotation is given.

But as our present condition can in no wise be shown inconsistent with the perfect moral government of God: so religion teaches us we were placed in it, that we might qualify ourselves, by the practice of virtue, for another state which is to follow it . . . .
. . . .
Every species of creatures, we see, designed for a particular way of life; to which, the nature, the capacities, temper, and qualifications of each species, are as necessary, as their external circumstances. Both come into the notion of such state, or particular way of life, and are constituent parts of it. Change a man's capacities or character to the degree, in which it is conceivable they may be changed; and he would be altogether incapable of a human course of life, and human happiness: as incapable, as if, his nature continuing unchanged, he were placed in a world, where he had no sphere of

action, nor any objects to answer his appetites, passions and affections of any sort. One thing is set over against another, as an ancient writer expresses it. Our nature corresponds to our external condition. Without this correspondence, there would be no possibility of any such thing as human life and human happiness: which life and happiness are, therefore, a *result* from our nature and condition jointly: meaning by human life, not living in the literal sense, but the whole complex notion commonly understood by those words.[6]

In Ramm's summary of A. E. Baker's thought on Butler, he brings out this idea of the unity of the universe and everything in it.

Butler took his cue from Newton and in terms of the natural, moral, and religious aspects of the universe and maintained that all was governed by one universal system or scheme of laws including all creatures in its comprehensiveness. The same general laws are exhibited in all domains of God's governance.[7]

Now what has all of this got to do with showing that Butler's ethic grows out of his theism? Just this: even if a person does not know the facts about man and the universe as outlined above, or, if knowing of them, still refuses to accept them as an accurate description of man and the universe, he may still be acting the same way as he would act if he knew and accepted this description. This is the case described by Paul in Romans 2:14-15 which Butler quotes in Sermon II. "For when the Gentiles, which have not the law, do by nature the things contained in the law, these, having not the law, are a law unto themselves: which shew the work of the law written in their hearts, their conscience also bearing witness, and their thought the meanwhile accusing or else excusing one another." The Gentiles who did not have the benefit of special revelation were conducting themselves according to this revelation because it was part of their inner nature.

Even if an individual is not aware of the theistic framework of the universe, he may still act according to it, if he is following his own nature to the fullest possible extent. If such is the case, the question could be asked, what is the advantage then of

---

[6] I, *Analogy*, Part I, chap. V, pp. 106-8, paras. 2 & 4.

[7] Ramm, *op. cit.*, p. 114.

knowing of the theistic framework? Butler does think that it is important for people who do not know to be told of it, as this is the direct implication of his Public Sermon I to the Society for the Propagation of the Gospel. Butler's answer to this question would most likely be that the individual would then know more of his obligations and thus be able to fulfill more of them.

Lefevre gives a summary statement which agrees with the contention that there is a unity throughout the universe, although he may not agree with the implication which has been drawn here.

From this may be inferred the true nature of Butler's metaphysics of ethics. While insisting that morality is grounded in human nature, and that its content is deducible from the structure of the self, he nevertheless holds that human nature has its place in the universe. Consequently, morality is in its last definition simply the 'eternal fitness' of things, and, like truth, is grounded in the nature of things. An examination into the 'nature of things' is, according to Butler . . . the other method by which the subject matter of ethics may be treated.[8]

Since God is the author of the nature of things, Butler's ethic grows out of his theism.

It should always be kept in mind that the *Analogy* is written as an apologetic against the deists. It has been noted that there are three basic tenets of theism. (1) There is a God. (2) The human individual is immortal. (3) Life in the future state is to some extent dependent upon the individual's conduct in the present state of existence. Since the deists as a group were not gathered into a school with a set doctrine but rather were a collection of independent thinkers, some of them might even agree with all three of these basic tenets of theism, so another criterion is needed to distinguish the deists from the theists. The real difference is that the deists maintained that in the act of creation God set the universe in operation according to natural laws and is no longer active in the universe, whereas the theists maintain that God may become active in the universe in some special manner, if he so chooses. The point of dispute between Butler and the deists was over the possibility of special revelation,

    [8] Albert Lefevre, "Conscience and Obligation in Butler's Ethical System", *Philosophical Review*, IX (July 1900), #52, p. 409.

which, of course, assumes a divine intervention in the natural course of the universe.

The deists maintained that man could find out all that he needed to know by the proper use of his reason; thus there was no need of special revelation. If a person were to read only Part I of the *Analogy,* it would seem that Butler had little quarrel with this position. In fact, theoretically, Butler had little quarrel with this position; but man lives in the realm of history, and not in the realm of theory. Because of his historical position, Butler had the advantage of special revelation which republishes all that man can know from natural revelation through the proper use of his reason, plus some new information. Since this was the case, it would have been the situation, if there were no special revelation. Butler takes a dim view of all such hypothetical pursuits.

This additional information contained in special revelation included at least these two statements; (1) man is in a state of corruption, and (2) man needs divine assistance from the second and third members of the godhead, the Son and Spirit, to lead him to salvation.

Christianity is not only an external institution of natural religion, and a new promulgation of God's general province, as righteous Governor and Judge of the world; but it contains also a revelation of a particular dispensation of Providence, carrying on by his Son and Spirit, for the recovery and salvation of mankind, who are represented, in scripture, to be in a state of ruin.[9]

The difficulty at this point is that Butler gives no reason why it is necessary for man to go beyond the information obtained from natural revelation to the additional information of special revelation. One of the basic presuppositions of natural religion is that man is quite capable of finding out what he needs to know by the proper use of his reason. If man were not corrupted, this would most likely be true, and the development in Part I of the *Analogy* of natural religion would be sufficient. It is true that Butler notes limitations of human reason as compared

---

[9] I, *Analogy*, Part I, chap. I, pp. 196-7, para. 16. Also I, "Introduction", p. 17, para. 16.

to the divine; but this follows from the metaphysical state of the creature and not from his corruption. But without special revelation, man would never know that he was corrupted and in need of divine assistance. This is the kind of hypothetical argument that Butler objects to, since it is concerned with what would have been the case, when the actual situation is different because man does have special revelation. The theoretical position is left in mid air; but this does not bother Butler, the practical churchman.

However, there seems to be an implicit switch from the theoretical possibility of knowledge of natural religion in Part I of the *Analogy* to the accepted historical event of special revelation of Part II. Butler was a practical man, and because of this fails to make the proper transition. Why discuss what would have been the case if there were no special revelation when as a matter of fact a special revelation has been given? Butler merely attempts to establish his stated purpose in the *Analogy,* which is to point out that the difficulties raised by the opponents of special revelation are analogous to difficulties found in the natural order of events. If a person is to be consistent, he cannot accept a divine author of the universe and reject a divine author of special revelation. Butler, of course, concludes that divine revelation is to be accepted, and in addition to the new information which it contains, it republishes the facts of natural religion.

The difference between theism and Christian theism is this additional information contained in special revelation. All of the three great historical systems of theism have their own special revelation. The Moslems have the Koran, the Jews have the Old Testament, and the Christians have both the Old Testament and the New Testament. Although it has been argued throughout this study that Butler was a theist, there seems to be no necessity in his thought for his being a Christian theist. He is, of course, a Christian by his own admission and by his inclusion of Part II of the *Analogy.* He is not driven to this position by the development of his argument; rather, he accepts the Christian revelation as a historical event and grafts it into his thought. Because of the great influence that Christian principles had on the cultural milieu of Butler's day, there was little difference between a

Christian and a non-Christian because of the state-church arrangement. The infant was born into the church and remained
in it whether or not he became an active Christian adult.

As a clergyman, Butler attempts to stimulate his people to
live more virtuous lives. In addition to the church as a Christian
community, they have the aid of special revelation which tells
of the Son and Spirit as well as reiterating the position of God
as Father. Butler's situation in life determined his approach. To
use a form of argument which he did not appreciate, it could be
said that if he had not been a Christian theist, he would not have
been a clergyman, and therefore, there would not have been the
Sermons. If he had not been a Christian apologist, there would
not have been the *Analogy*.

In a religious ethic it is difficult to differentiate between ethics
and religion. Butler has no interest in this distinction. His objective was to stimulate people to virtuous living, and he used every
means available. Today it is commonly held that there are three
general answers which can be given to the question of how man
should act, and it should be interesting to see how Butler fits
into this classification. As it was noted in Chapter I above,
Weaver has pointed out that there are tendencies in Butler toward
each of these three answers. (1) Man should act on the principle
of pleasure so that the most pleasure will be obtained for himself
or for all humans involved. (2) Man should act so as to realize
the highest potentialities for his own human nature or for the
nature of all humans concerned. Both of these first two alternatives are teleological in that the action is based on the consequences which will result from that action. (3) The last alternative is deontological in that the individual should act according
to his duty without concern for the consequences. In addition to
deciding which of these principles is to be accepted as the guide
for action, there is the epistemological problem of how the individual knows how he should act.

(1) The pleasure principle is included in Butler's thought
through his two principles of human nature of self-love and
benevolence. Self-love, the egoistic aspect, and benevolence, the
universal aspect, are held by Butler to be complimentary and not

competing principles. In fact, the individual's own pleasure will not be fulfilled unless he is concerned for others. (2) The self-realization aspect is included through the concept that the individual and his circumstances have been so arranged by God that man is at home in the universe. Furthermore, man is in a state of probation so that it is possible for him to develop his potentialities. Since it is man's moral nature which differentiates him from all other creatures, this is the aspect to be cultivated. As long as man is by nature a man, he will act like a man; but the individual may develop himself by attempting to approximate the ideal man of Jesus Christ. (3) The duty aspect of conduct is most clearly expressed by Butler in the "Dissertation on Virtue"; but the current runs throughout his writings. It is so strong in the "Dissertation" that sometimes Butler is classified along with Kant on the basis of it. In general, there is an acknowledged standard of virtue, and it is man's duty to follow this standard. It turns out for Butler that man obtains pleasure and develops himself by acting virtuously; but the emphasis of the "Dissertation" is that it is man's duty to so act. It seems that any Christian theistic approach to ethics will contain elements of all three, although one may be predominant. The predominant aspect in Butler will vary, depending upon what part of his writings are being considered. Because of his organic conception of the universe, it is possible to begin with any aspect and arrive at the same conclusion.

When it comes to discussing the means by which man knows how he should act, Butler again had several available. (1) God has given man a conscience by which he can determine what he should do. Conscience has been placed within man by God, and this is what makes man a moral creature. The way that the conscience functions should determine whether Butler is to be classified with the rationalists or with the moral sense theorists. If Butler holds that man reasons to the virtue or vice in a situation, then he is a rationalist; if he holds that man immediately feels the virtue or vice of the situation, then he espouses a moral sense. The problem here is that Butler does not state which he is, and perhaps this is his main deficiency as an ethical theorist.

Moreover, he is unconcerned with this distinction. In the "Dissertation on Virtue" he says that a "great part of common language, and of common behaviour over the world, is formed upon supposition of such a moral faculty; whether called conscience, moral reason, moral sense, or divine reason; whether considered as a sentiment of the understanding, or a perception of the heart; or, which seems the truth, as including both".[10] Taylor is not so harsh in his criticism: Butler "avoided taking up any definite position, and, as I have said, I think him justified on the ground that, for his immediate purpose, which is simply to insist on the authority of the moral law, a discussion of the precise way in which the law is apprehended would be irrelevant and disturbing".[11] This study does agree with Taylor that Butler was a rationalist in the sense that "the intellect can apprehend principles which are implied in and justify our approbation and disapprobation".[12]

(2) If a man looks within himself and properly understands his constitution and looks without and understands his environment, he will realize that his nature is adapted to its situation. The study of man will indicate that there is a hierarchy of principles, and when man follows his inclinations in the measure allowed by any one of these principles, he sees how he should act. Conscience is the voice of God within man,[13] so supposedly there is no problem with the reliability of this principle. If self-love or benevolence is followed, the individual will also act as he should. A proper understanding of the passions will lead to the conclusion that they should be under the control of the higher principles; so again, by following his own nature, man will act properly.

(3) If an individual wants an external authority to tell him how he should act, God has also provided for this situation. The primary means of external authority is through the Christian scriptures, which for Butler constitute special revelation. All that

---

[10] I, "Dissertation on Virtue", p. 399, para. 2.
[11] Taylor, *op. cit.*, p. 298.
[12] *Ibid.*, p. 299.
[13] I, "Introduction to the Analogy", p. 15, para. 13.

man has to do is to follow the instructions contained in scripture, and he will act as he should act. The church, which is the witness to this revelation continuing in history, is another means of external authority.

(4) The last means to be mentioned is the pleasure-pain principle. God has so constituted the universe that he has affixed pleasurable consequences to the actions that man ought to do and painful consequences to the actions that man ought not to do. Man may be kept from doing a vicious act in a manner similar to a burn resulting from contact with fire, by an uneasy feeling such as that of guilt, or by the pressures of society. Therefore, if a man pursues the actions which give pleasurable consequences and shuns those which cause pain, he will be acting the way that he should act. There is, of course, the possibility of perversion connected with each of these possibilities, but if they are followed in a natural sense, man will be acting the way that he should act.

As this study is brought to a close, it is found that the reader is left unsure of Butler's position on important questions that should be answered in an ethical system, but nevertheless persuaded that his ethic is connected to his theology. Perhaps the title of ethical theorist has been loosely applied to Butler, and rather, he should more accurately be called a moral preacher. Taylor pointed out above that Butler's purpose was "simply to insist on the authority of the moral law".[14] No one questions his intention of exhorting people to live virtuously; but this does not necessarily imply a theory behind the exhortations. What there is of an ethical theory is not clearly presented in his writings. Perhaps Norton is right when he says that Butler caught a vision.

His insight into the nature of the universe with its spiritual basis in the mind of God is more certain and more real to him than any arguments that lead to its establisment for us . . . It is this undercurrent of vision that Butler never doubts or foresakes.[15]

[14] Taylor, *op. cit.*, p. 298.
[15] Norton, *op. cit.*, p. 214.

BIBLIOGRAPHY

BOOKS

Abbey, Charles J., and Overton, John H., *The English Church in the Eighteenth Century*. Revised and Abridged (London, Longmans, Green & Co., 1896).

Anthony Earl of Shaftesbury, *Characteristics of Men, Manners, Opinions, Times, Etc.* Edited by John M. Robertson (London, Grant Richards, 1900).

Bartlett, Thomas, *Memoirs of the Life, Character, and Writings of Joseph Butler* (London, John W. Parker, 1839).

Broad, C. D., *Five Types of Ethical Theory* (New York, Harcourt, Brace & Co., 1930).

Butler, Joseph, *Works*. Edited by J. H. Bernard. 2 vols. (London, Macmillan & Co., Ltd., 1900).

——, *Works*. Edited by W. E. Gladstone. 2 vols. (Oxford, At the Clarendon Press, 1896).

——, *Works*. Edited by Samuel Halifax (New York, Robert Caster, 1846).

Clarke, Samuel, *A Discourse Concerning the Being and Attributes of God, the Obligations of Natural Religion, and the Truth and Certainty of the Christian Revelation*. 6th ed. (London, James Knapton, 1725).

Cudworth, Ralph, *The True Intellectual System of the Universe*. Translated by J. Harrison. Vol. III. *A Treatise Concerning Eternal and Immutable Morality*. (London, Thomas Tegg, 1845).

Cumberland, Richard, *A Treatise on the Laws of Nature*. Translated by John Maxwell (London, R. Phillips, 1727).

Duncan-Jones, Austin, *Butler's Moral Philosophy* (Harmondsworth, Penguin Books, 1952).

Eggleston, William Morley, *Stanhope Memorials of Bishop Butler* (London, Simpkin, Marshall & Co., 1878).

Freud, Sigmund, *New Introductory Lectures on Psycho-Analysis* (New York, W. W. Norton & Co., Inc., 1933).

Galloway, George, *Faith and Reason in Religion*. (New York, Charles Scribner's Sons, 1928).

Gladstone, W. E., *Studies Subsidiary to the Works of Bishop Butler* (New York, Macmillan & Co., 1896).

Hobbes, Thomas, *Leviathan* (Oxford, At the Clarendon Press, 1909).

Hutcheson, Frances, *An Inquiry into the Original of our Ideas of Beauty and Virtue.* Treatise II (London, J. Darby, 1725).

Leland, John, *A View of the Principle Deistical Writers.* Introduction by Cyrus R. Edmonds (London, T. Tegg & Son, 1837).

Locke, John, *An Essay Concerning Human Understanding.* 16th ed. (London, (no publisher), 1768).

——, *Essays on the Law of Nature.* Edited by W. Von Leyden (Oxford, At the Clarendon Press, 1954).

Mandeville, Bernard, *The Fable of the Bees.* Edited by D. Garman (London, Wishert & Co., 1934).

More, Henry, *Enchiridion Ethicum.* English translation of 1960 (New York, Facsimile Text Society, 1930).

Mossner, Ernest C., *Bishop Butler and the Age of Reason* (New York, Macmillan Co., 1936).

New Letters of David Hume. Edited by Raymond Klibansky and Ernest C. Mossner (Oxford, At the Clarendon Press, 1954).

Norton, William J., *Bishop Butler: Moralist and Divine* (New Brunswick, Rutgers University Press, 1940).

Prichard, H. A., *Duty and Interest* (Oxford, University Press, 1928).

Ramm, Bernard, *Types of Apologetic Systems* (Wheaton, Van Kampen Press, Inc., 1953).

Rand, Benjamin, *The Classical Moralists* (Boston, Houghton-Mifflin Co., 1909).

Rogers, A. K., *Morals in Review* (New York, Macmillan Co., 1927).

Rogers, Reginald A. P., *A Short History of Ethics* (London, Macmillan & Co., 1952).

Selby-Bigge, L. A., *British Moralists.* 2 vols. (Oxford, At the Clarendon Press, 1897).

Sidgwick, Henry, *Outlines of the History of Ethics.* 6th ed. (London, Macmillan & Co., 1954).

Spooner, W. A., *Bishop Butler* (Boston, Houghton, Mifflin & Co., 1901).

Stephen, Leslie, *History of English Thought in the Eighteenth Century.* 2 vols. 3rd ed. (New York, Peter Smith, 1949).

Taylor, A. E., *Philosophical Studies* (London, Macmillan & Co., Ltd., 1934).

Tindal, Matthew, *Christianity as Old as the Creation: or the Gospel, a Republication of the Religion of Nature* (Newburgh, David Denniston, 1748).

Weaver, Oliver C. Jr., "Duty and Purpose in the Ethical Theory of Joseph Butler". Unpublished Ph. D. dissertation, Department of Philosophy, Northwestern University, 1952.

Wollaston, William, *The Religion of Nature Delineated.* 5th ed. (London, James & John Knopton, 1731).

ARTICLES

Bernard, J. H., "The Predecessors of Bishop Butler", *Hermathena,* IX (1896).

Broad, C. D., "Butler as a Theologian", *Hibbert Journal,* XXI (July, 1923).

Goligher, William A., "Butler's Indebtedness to Aristotle", *Hermathena*, XII (1903).

Grove, S. A., "The Foundation of Butler's Ethics", *The Australasian Journal of Philosophy*, XXX (August, 1952).

Jackson, Reginald, "Bishop Butler's Refutation of Psychological Hedonism," *Philosophy*, XVIII (July, 1943).

Kyle, W. M., "British Ethical Theories — The Importance of Butler", *The Australasian Journal of Psychology and Philosophy*, VII (December, 1929).

Lefevre, Albert, "Self Love and Benevolence in Butler's Ethical System", *Philosophical Review*. IX (March, 1900).

——, "The Significance of Butler's View of Human Nature", *Philosophical Review*, VIII (March, 1899).

——, "Conscience and Obligation in Butler's Ethical System", *Philosophical Review*, IX (July, 1900).

McPherson, Thomas H., "The Development of Bishop Butler's Ethics", Part I, *Philosophy*, XXIII (October, 1948).

——, "The Development of Bishop Butler's Ethics", Part II, *Philosophy*, January, 1949.

Purser, Frederick, "Butler's Indebtedness to Aristotle: A Reply", *Hermathena*, XII (1903).

Raphael, D. Daiches, "Bishop Butler's View of Conscience", *Philosophy*, XXIV (July, 1949).

Townsend, H. G., "The Synthetic Principle in Butler's Ethics", *International Journal of Ethics*, XXXVII (October, 1926).